MW00669345

CRAFTING DEVOTIONS

CRAFTING DEVOTIONS

....

TRADITION IN CONTEMPORARY NEW MEXICO SANTOS

LAURIE BETH KALB

PHOTOGRAPHS BY

MARY PECK, MIGUEL A. GANDERT, AND SUSAN EINSTEIN

UNIVERSITY OF NEW MEXICO PRESS

ALBUQUERQUE

in association with

GENE AUTRY WESTERN HERITAGE MUSEUM

LOS ANGELES

Copyright © 1994 by the University of New Mexico Press.

All rights reserved.

First edition

Library of Congress Cataloging-in-Publication Data

Kalb, Laurie Beth.

Crafting devotions: tradition in contemporary New Mexico Santos /
Laurie Beth Kalb; photographs by Mary Peck, Miguel A Gandert, and
Susan Einstein. —1st ed.

p.   cm.

Includes bibliographical references and index.

ISBN 0-8263-1549-6 (cl).— ISBN 0-0263-1550-X (pa)

1. Santos (Art) —New Mexico—. 2 Hispanic American art— New
Mexico. 3. Folk art—New Mexico —History—20th century. I Title.

NK835.N5K36 1994   94-28253

704.9'482—dc20   CIP

Printed in Hong Kong

Cover: Bulto of Nuestra Señora del Carmen (Our Lady of Mt. Carmel),
1992, by Victor Goler. Fig. 4

Page 1: Wooden head for Santos, by Enrique Rendón. Fig. 113.

Page 2: Bulto of Nuestra Señora de Guadalupe, by Felix López.Detail of Fig. 109.

Page 4: Bulto of San Miguel Archángel, 1971, by George Lopez. Detail of Fig. 3

For the woodcarvers and their families

CONTENTS

FOREWORD

THE REGION WHICH MOST PEOPLE THINK OF as the West is one which has been viewed through the eyes of many cultures over a period of centuries. Indeed, the concept of a "West" is one which has been constructed in relatively recent times from the attitudes and views of the dominant Anglo American society. From its inception in 1984 and since its opening in the fall of 1988, the Gene Autry Western Heritage Museum has pursued a mission which demands a closer view of that West and an examination of the perceptions and experiences of all groups in the region. By expanding the temporal, geographic, and topical parameters of Western studies we attempt to delve more deeply into the traditions, experiences, history, and art of the many immigrant and resident peoples who have inhabited the region.

A primary tool of interpretive programs, exhibitions, and collections strategies for the institution has been the utilization of multi-disciplinary approaches to the assessment of the past. In 1990 the Museum began more formally to develop its collection of arts and cultural materials reflecting the traditions and lives of the peoples of the West. In that year Dr. Laurie Beth Kalb joined the staff as curator of folk art bringing the insights of folk material culture studies and the discipline of folklore more effectively into our programs. Added to the expertise of staff with backgrounds in history and anthropology, this productive combination allowed the institution's efforts to expand and grow. With publication of *Crafting Devotions: Tradition in Contemporary New Mexico Santos*, and release of its related exhibition, we are happy to acknowledge the personal devotion and commitment of the book's author. Laurie Beth Kalb has moved on to new professional challenges, but the institution's commitment to growth of the collection and the development of interpretive programs continues. The Gene Autry Western Heritage Museum was formed to serve as an institution of breadth and quality, devoted to preserving and exploring the broadest parameters of the heritage of a region. As so amply demonstrated by this volume, that effort is meant to be inclusive and insightful.

JOANNE D. HALE
Chief Executive Officer and Director
JAMES H. NOTTAGE
Chief Curator
Gene Autry Western Heritage Museum, Los Angeles

9

PREFACE

M Y FIRST IMPRESSION of New Mexico, in summer 1983, remains my most vivid. A graduate student in folklore and folklife at the University of Pennsylvania, I came to New Mexico to intern at the Museum of International Folk Art. I was hired to research that institution's holdings in Greek material culture, specifically religious votives, a subject I had studied before. Excited about my summer job, I was also thrilled by the adventure of encountering New Mexico. I had never been that far west.

A roommate from a college semester I spent in Greece, Dessa Bokides Fay, then living in New Mexico, picked me up at the airport. On our drive north from Albuquerque to Santa Fe, I noticed something large, lightweight, and gray roll across the highway, intruding, I thought, on a pristine and majestic landscape before us. Remarking how, even in the West, trash litters the roads, I betrayed my decidedly East Coast and urban worldview. Rather than garbage rolling across the road, my amused yet patient friend explained, sagebrush had tumbled along.

By the end of that summer, I learned something about New Mexico's flora and fauna, but even more about the value of a community's ideals. In a newly purchased used car, I drove north, along the banks of the Rio Grande, toward the southern foot of the Rocky Mountains, meeting members of the towns and villages there, and getting to know a cultural and geographical landscape that almost immediately, quite profoundly, took hold of me. Abandoning my project of studying Greek folk art, located in the museum's basement, I chose instead to learn what I could about santos, Hispano Catholic images of saints first introduced to the northern frontier of New Spain, now New Mexico, by sixteenth- and seventeenth-century Spanish settlers. As I visited various towns and villages, I learned that a growing number of local carvers and painters, impassioned by the artistry and history of Spanish colonial crafts, were making new santos, in many cases fashioning them on the style of older works. With each artist I met, I learned about yet another local person, studying the region's past and skillfully producing religious objects.

The fine scholarship of E. Boyd, William Wroth, José E. Espinosa, and Thomas J. Steele, S. J. taught me a great deal about the history and aesthetics of Spanish colonial santos. In the eighteenth and nineteenth centuries, in an effort to replenish a dwindling supply of religious goods originally provided by the Spanish crown, settlers carved and painted santos out of local wood and minerals. They relied on both their immediate harsh surroundings and a transcendent spirituality to make much-needed religious goods. In their symmetry, these santos dispensed with academic conventions and moved to abstraction, a style that, in the Middle Ages, was motivated by common Purpose.

Although Spanish colonial santos were mostly unsigned, Spanish colonial folk art scholars established various painting and carving styles for them, identified anonymous artists, and suggested a functional value for santos in history. Still, as these studies relied only slightly on local people for information, they neglected folk memory, a valuable resource for understanding the meaning of santos in contemporary as well as historic communities. Generally, Spanish colonial folk art scholars dismissed twentieth-century woodcarving, considering it inferior in quality and inauthentic compared to older images.

I turned to Charles L. Briggs, who showed how santo making continued in the early and mid-twentieth century, years after its religious necessity dwindled, owing to the introduction of mass-produced images. Still, Briggs, who wrote his book in the 1970s, treated only one style of carving from one village, motivated primarily by two complementary influences—tourism and a local community's urgent need for cash income. In the early 1980s, when I first came to New Mexico, the Córdova style of carving Briggs so admirably described persisted, but, as Briggs also mentioned, alongside of a burgeoning woodcarving activity that had as much to do with political, religious, and aesthetic empowerment as it did with marketing.

This book grew out of extensive fieldwork I conducted between 1983 and 1992 among northern New Mexico santeros (makers of saints), that resulted in my doctoral dissertation. I focus on a contemporary carving scene that recalls santo making of the Spanish colonial period and the late-nineteenth through mid-twentieth centuries, but that lives because of woodcarvers' complicated interactions with present influences. My focus is the present. I refer to santeros of the past if they have particular meaning for contemporary carvers. I step into history and tradition as it is being constructed, revived, or reinvented by living, vital artists.

Throughout this project, I established close ties with many people. Since 1983, four famous woodcarvers—Enrique Rendón, Leo Salazar, Horacio Valdéz, and George López—died. I miss these old men, but cherish the time I had with them. In my fieldwork, I grew especially close to Enrique Rendón. After Enrique died, perhaps through a shared sense of loss, his partner, Margaret Gutierrez, his sister, Dulcinea López, and I became close friends. To offer these women special thanks seems woefully inadequate.

Early in my research, as a graduate student, I had the great benefit of discussing santos and art with Henry Glassie. His support has been constant and inspirational. Roger Abrahams, Charles L. Briggs, Burt Feintuch, Kenneth S. Goldstein, Barbara Kirshenblatt-Gimblett, Robert Blair St. George, Marta Weigle, and Don Yoder read, commented on, and otherwise responded to the research and writing that became this book. I owe much to these scholars, although I take full responsibility for the words on these pages.

Many museum mentors, colleagues, and friends contributed generously. I am grateful to Richard E. Ahlborn, Charmay Allred, Teresa Archuleta-Sagel, Raymond Bal and Elizabeth Kay, Elma Bal, Jonathan Batkin, Joan Benedetti, Dessa Bokides Fay, Charlene Cerny, Andrew Connors, Mary Pat Day, Ray Dewey, Patrick H. Ela, Carl Fleischhauer, Robin Farwell Gavin, Joanne D. Hale, Linda Roscoe Hartigan, Bud and Barbara Hoover, Marsha Jackson, Tracy Adair Jaramillo, Ellen Landis, Yvonne Lange, Mark Lewis, Vicente Martínez, Timothy Maxwell, Thomas Merlan, Kevin Mulroy, Mary Ellen Hennessey Nottage, Nat Owings, Diana Pardue, Neil Poese, Bud Redding, Kate Sibley, Lonn Taylor,

David Turner, Robert and Ruth Vogele, Alfred J. Walker, and David Witt. Charlene Cerny, my first boss in New Mexico, provided special help in the early stages of this work. Years later, in 1990, a Smithsonian Institution graduate fellowship enabled me to take a leave from curating and begin writing my dissertation. Richard Ahlborn supervised this grant. He and Lonn Taylor offered time, support, and their great knowledge of the material culture of the American West.

Mary Peck, Miguel A. Gandert, and Susan Einstein took beautiful photographs. Mary Peck has worked on two santo projects with me, sharing her affection for the santeros as well as her great skill.

Special thanks are due to Dana Asbury of the University of New Mexico Press; James Nottage and John Langellier of the Gene Autry Western Heritage Museum; and Dana Levy of Perpetua Press—colleagues, and now friends, responsible for the fine production of this book amidst long-distance transmittals from me.

My parents and stepparents, Saundra and George Segan Wheeler and Gerald and Mary Kalb, visited New Mexico, offering enthusiasm and love for a place and a project that mean so much to me. In various ways, Barbara Baker, Martha Bustin, Martha and Rainer Frost, Robert A. Hill, Michael Holt, Susan L. F. Isaacs, Emily Kalb, Jonathan Kalb and Julie Heffernan, Mario Montaño, and Leonard Primiano gave encouragement and friendship.

Finally, I must thank the artists and their families: Luis Barela, Jr., Charles M. and Debbie Carrillo, Marie Romero Cash, Gloria López Córdova, Victor Goler, Edward González, Nicolás Herrera, Eddie Johnson, Lori Johnson, Félix and Louise López, José Benjamín and Irene López, Ramón José López, Luisito Luján, Eluid Levi Martínez, Wilberto Miera, Eulogio and Zoraida Ortega, Sabinita López Ortíz, Marco and Patricia Oviedo, Orlando Romero, José Roybal, Luis Tapia, and Irvin and Lisa Trujillo. They may think they taught me just about santos, but that was only the beginning.

CRAFTING DEVOTIONS

INTRODUCTION

CRAFTING DEVOTIONS

L A FONDA HOTEL'S BALLROOM was full of saints. Carved or painted, they lay on tables. Anglo and Hispano tourists, dealers, curators, and artists mixed inside Santa Fe's old tourist hotel, previewing the next day's market. Everywhere I looked, they were talking, browsing, judging, displaying, dealing. Once again, it was the Friday evening of July's last weekend, and Spanish Market Preview was in full swing. For me it was one of the high points of the year.

I came to Santa Fe from Los Angeles, California, where I was curator of folk art for the Gene Autry Western Heritage Museum. I was working on an exhibition and developing a collection of contemporary New Mexico santos. Santos, or Hispano-Catholic religious images, are a key material expression of Hispano New Mexican culture. Sixteenth-century Spanish colonists originally brought santos for devotional use to what are now the Americas. Early on, local settlers also produced their own santos to fill a void left by the withdrawal of Spanish ecclesiastical authorities from northern New Spain. Today, craftspeople make religious images for political, aesthetic, and marketing purposes as well as for holy needs. Santos take two forms—three-dimensional bultos, or carved wooden sculptures, and flat paintings on pine boards, called retablos. The altar screens that santeros, or saint makers, produce for mission churches and smaller chapels are called reredos.

The Spanish Market Preview inaugurates the midsummer weekend when Hispano New Mexican santeros, furniture makers, weavers, and tin workers sell their wares to a predominantly outsider—or Anglo—clientele. For the preview, officers of the Spanish Colonial Arts Society (SCAS), the mostly Anglo

Fig. 1. Retablo of Nuestra Señora de los Dolores (Our Lady of Sorrows), ca. 1790, by Laguna Santero. Collection: Gene Autry Western Heritage Museum. Photo: Susan Einstein.

15

preservationist organization that sponsors Spanish Market, invite artists to exhibit their two most treasured works before bringing them to market the next morning. From these displays, SCAS judges select award-winning pieces. Judges' criteria include aesthetic excellence, technical skill, and adherence to SCAS board members' notions of Spanish colonial tradition.

Especially in New Mexico, native attitudes toward ethnic identity and tradition often differ from popular images of Southwestern culture. In its local connotation, tradition is a series of cultural traits that invoke the past. Such an interpretation is frequently used in the service of cultural authenticity, a validation, following folklorist Henry Glassie, based on preserving lines of communication between generations and a persistence of practice despite change.[1] In academic contexts, some contemporary scholars attempt to wrest tradition away from such formulations, arguing that it is symbolically constructed, that "tradition" is a recasting of the past, created in the present.[2] In New Mexico, a rhetoric of tradition figures in the lived experience of all. Santeros, in particular, appropriate it for themselves. Today, like scholars, makers of saints and other carvings debate the meaning of tradition; for them, this connects powerfully to cultural self-representation. In New Mexico, among all who make, sell, and display santos, the politics of identity, tradition, and culture remains complex and very strong.

For Spanish Colonial Arts Society board members, making traditional crafts means adhering to the Spanish colonial style developed by SCAS, that is, replicating nineteenth-century religious and domestic items found in museums, private collections, and some churches, and also perpetuating a revival style begun in the 1920s in response to early Anglo patrons. These Anglo newcomers encouraged the production of new statues, Hispano furniture, and other wood carvings fashioned loosely on the styles of old images but left unpainted to suit their own aesthetics.[3] For some contemporary carvers, the SCAS notion of tradition, which includes the early patrons' selective criteria, is too limited. It does not embrace today's carvers' innovative stylistic preferences.

The official rules of the Spanish Colonial Arts Society prevent artists from selling their works during the preview. This is a night for displaying art and celebrating awards, not vending. In many instances at the preview, artists do not even stand alongside their creations, making business transactions difficult, if not impossible.

Nevertheless, sales are a major aspect of the Spanish Market Preview. Unofficial negotiations between patrons and artists prevail. A veteran Spanish Market-goer, I was acutely aware of the potential for unauthorized transactions during the preview. For this reason, in the summer of 1992, I went to New Mexico a few days before the preview, hoping to see new works before they even made their way to market. My mission was a success; I arrived at the preview with one purchase already in mind. That night, the piece I wanted, a skillfully carved, painted, and varnished bulto of Nuestra Señora del Carmen (Our Lady of Mt. Carmel), made to resemble Spanish colonial images, became a grand prize winner. Victor Goler, a young rising star among santeros, was the artist.

I knew that Goler's award meant that competition for buying his work would intensify. It also heightened my interest in acquiring the piece for the museum. The grand prize officially sanctioned the santo's exceptional quality and its rightful place in a museum collection. However, I also knew that Goler honored the rules of the preview and would not sell his work until early the next

PREVIOUS PAGES

Left

Fig. 2. Bulto of San Ysidro Labradór (Saint Isidore the Farmer), ca. 1890, by José Benito Ortega. Collection: Gene Autry Western Heritage Museum. Photo: Susan Einstein

Right.

Fig. 3. Bulto of San Miguel Arcángel (Saint Michael the Archangel), 1971, by George López. Collection: Gene Autry Western Heritage Museum. Donative purchase from Eluid Levi Martinez. Photo: Susan Einstein.

Fig. 4. Bulto of Nuestra Señora del Carmen
(Our Lady of Mt. Carmel), 1992, by Victor
Goler. Blue ribbon for first place in the santo
category, 1992 Spanish Market. Maroon
ribbon for grand prize, 1992 Spanish
Market. Collection: Gene Autry Western
Heritage Museum. Photo: Susan Einstein.

Fig. 5. Victor Goler in his Taos studio, 1992. The early Taos painter Joseph Sharp had this large adobe structure built for him as a studio in 1918. Victor Goler has lived and worked in this building for the past six years. Photo: Mary Peck.

Fig. 6. Chess set, 1992, by Marie Romero Cash, wood, acrylics, tin, magnets, 28" x 25 3/4" x 25 1/2". With the exception of the rooks, carved as three-tiered cylindrical buildings, all the chess figures have frontal forms and are painted like santos. The queens wear gowns and crowns, holding their hands is if praying, akin to images of the Virgin. The kings are bearded, wear long robes, and hold a red flower in their right hands and a child in their left. They resemble images of San José (Saint Joseph). Collection: Gene Autry Western Heritage Museum. Photo: Susan Einstein.

morning, when the market formally began. Not wanting to lose sight of other opportunities, I moved away from Goler's exhibit and walked around the ballroom, looking for other works of interest.

A carved and polychromed chess set with figures fashioned as saints caught my eye. The chessboard formed the top of a table; its side shelves were painted with Indian symbols of a moon and sun. Because of the table's height, the chess set had a visual presence unrivaled by anything else in the room. Interested buyers already hovered over it. The stunning santo chess set was a particularly creative response to the heightened influence that outsider patrons can have on objects produced for market. Chess sets have no precedent at Spanish Market, making this one questionable, yet piquing my curatorial interest. I wanted this work for my show and for the museum collection. I knew the artist, Marie Romero Cash, so I set out find her.

Spanish Market first began in the 1920s, developing out of the revival efforts of Anglo artist and writer Frank Applegate and Anglo writer Mary Austin, who founded the Spanish Colonial Arts Society. Formed for the purpose of reviving local handicrafts, Spanish Market was created by SCAS to display and sell crafts during the Santa Fe Fiesta. In addition, the Spanish Colonial Arts Society held prize competitions among Hispano craftspeople and established a Spanish Arts Shop in Santa Fe's Sena Plaza.[4] The market continued annually until the mid-1930s, resuming its annual ritual in 1965. In 1985, activist, artist, and librarian Orlando Romero and others created a Contemporary Hispano Market that took place at the same time as Spanish Market in an enclosed patio at the state history museum in downtown Santa Fe. Intended to complement the traditional Spanish Market, the Contemporary Hispano Market provided artists a less-constrained arena in which to exhibit their works. The Contemporary Market proved successful, and in 1990 its organizers moved it to Lincoln Avenue, a more visible location adjacent to the plaza where the traditional market takes place. In the 1980s, Spanish Market became so popular that in 1989 a second venue was established, a Winter Market held every December in La Fonda Hotel.

By seven o'clock the Saturday morning after the preview, an hour before Spanish Market was to begin, my museum was the owner of three new santos. At the preview's end, I had found Marie Cash, who agreed to sell me her chess set the following day. On Saturday morning, I came to the plaza at 6:30, vying for Goler's Nuestra Señora del Carmen. Goler had not yet appeared, so I looked around to see who was there. The grounds were quiet, with artists setting up their booths and a few serious collectors looking for the artists whose works they wanted to buy. A man who reached the plaza before me, an art dealer from Boston, was also waiting for Goler. Two days earlier, when visiting Goler in his studio, I had learned about this man. An owner of other examples of the young artist's work, he had called Goler a few months before market to ask if the artist could make a carving of the Pietà. Goler had never made a Pietà. This particular image of Mary mourning over the body of Christ in her arms is not common in New Mexico. Our Lady of Sorrows, or Mary with a sword or seven swords piercing her heart, is a more typical depiction of the grieving Virgin.[5] Goler liked the challenge of making something new, but he would not promise the bulto to the collector before the market. I felt sure that as the market began he would sell the art dealer whatever bulto or retablo he wanted. On the other hand, the Boston art dealer had heard I was from a West Coast museum. He was con-

Fig. 7. Bulto of Pietà, 1992, by Victor Goler.
Collection: Alfred Walker. Photo: Mary Peck.

vinced he had no chance of acquiring the work he had asked the santero to craft. Certain that we were competing, we waited anxiously and quietly. After a few minutes, Goler's fiancée, now his wife, and her mother arrived. Then Goler walked in. I spoke up first, asking for Nuestra Señora del Carmen. The man from Boston immediately asked for the Pietà. I put down a cash deposit, took my receipt and remaining bill, and breathed a huge sigh of relief.

While waiting for Goler to arrive at the market, at 6:30, I ran into another santero, my old friend, Horacio Valdez, who would die several weeks later. Self-taught and highly skilled, Valdez had achieved international recognition for his wood carvings. That summer, the Spanish Colonial Arts Society designated Valdez and another master carver, Luisito Luján, honored artists at the market. Unlike other participants who paid a fee for a booth and brought their works to market to sell, Valdez and Luján came to the market as guests, to exhibit their art. Their work was officially not for sale. Luján, who has made painted santos since the 1970s, had never participated in Spanish Market. A deeply spiritual man who believes in expressive freedom for Hispano artists and disagrees with the notion of tradition espoused by SCAS board members, Luján sells his works from his home.

Horacio Valdez, also very religious, once sold his painted santos at market but stopped a few years ago. Along with Luis Tapia and Orlando Romero, Valdez, a retired carpenter, was among the first santeros to introduce painted santos into Spanish Market in the 1970s. Before then, artists left their carvings unpainted, following the style of the 1920s revival. Ethnic awareness led contemporary carvers to begin applying color to their images. They reached back to the expressive forms of the Spanish colonial period, when santos were polychrome, rather than to the early-twentieth-century revival, to craft their own versions of tradition. Valdez's decision to curtail participation in the market had less to do with ethnic politics than with practicality, however. The artist simply had too many "orders," or commissions, from private collectors. He had no time to produce a cache of santos to sell at Spanish Market.

Although I knew that Valdez rarely had extra santos available, I took a chance and asked if he had anything for sale. To my surprise, he said that a couple of the pieces he brought had not yet sold. Did I want to have a look? Seeing that Goler had not yet arrived, I quickly agreed. We walked to his car, where he opened the trunk and uncovered at least half a dozen wood carvings. Two santos were available. I immediately fixed on one of them, a brilliantly polychromed image of San Miguel Arcángel (Saint Michael the Archangel), patron of soldiers, guardian of small children, and opponent of the devil and all evil. In this piece, Valdez had achieved a beautiful harmony of bright colors, using acrylics. The rough texture on the dragon's body emphasized an exceptionally smooth finish on the archangel. The dragon's human face added to the piece's compelling force. Without considering my other purchasing plans, I sim-

Fig. 8. Horacio Valdez in his studio, Apodaca, 1984. A well-known photograph of Taos woodcarver Patrocinio Barela with one of his carvings hangs on the wall behind Valdez. Courtesy American Folklife Center, Library of Congress. Photo: Carl Fleischhauer.

Fig. 9. Luisito Luján with an unfinished wood carving of La Virgen (The Virgin), Nambé, 1992. Photo: Mary Peck.

Overleaf

Left

Fig. 10. Bulto of La Sagrada Familia (Holy Family) in carved *nicho* (niche), by Luisito Luján. Collection of the artist. Photo: Mary Peck.

Right

Fig. 11. Bulto of San Miguel Arcángel, 1992, by Horacio Valdez. Collection: Gene Autry Western Heritage Museum. Photo: Susan Einstein.

ply told Valdez I would buy his piece. Because he knew me, the artist had no need of a deposit. He would wait for a check from the museum.

There was still an hour before the official opening of the market. Having arranged the business of my three acquisitions—Cash's chess set, Valdez's San Miguel, and Goler's Pietà—and having spent 10,000 dollars, I walked around the plaza, viewing the range of other crafts for sale. A handwritten sign reading Sold to the Museum appeared in front of Marie Cash's chess set. At market, when artworks sell to museums, artists often place the business card of the professional who purchases the piece alongside of the work. Just as blue ribbon prizes awarded by SCAS judges gain artworks prestige and affirmation, so does a museum acquisition. At Spanish Market, santeros do more than display and sell their wood carvings; through their sales, they exhibit their economic and artistic success as well as their affiliations with cultural institutions. Curators and other art world professionals who place their business cards next to their purchases leave their judgment open to public scrutiny. Spanish Market is an event shared by artists, collectors, museum personnel, and tourists. Everyone is on display. Increasingly, as prices of Hispano crafts rise, tourists are excluded from this performance. As the late curator George Mills noted for santos in museums, Spanish Market santos, divorced from their religious use and staged within a framework of tradition, heritage, and professional culture, confuse rather than clarify the nature of Spanish-American life in New Mexico.[6]

Like the notion of tradition itself, Spanish Market is controversial among New Mexico Hispano artists. Because the criteria for entry include adherence to tradition as defined by an essentially Anglo board, contemporary santeros

vary in how much they participate. This has been especially true in the last twenty years, when issues of ethnic awareness have caused members of minorities to reassess the dominant Anglo culture, especially as it relates to the fine art world and tourism. In some instances, Hispanos, mostly men, have become santeros as a means of ethnic and political self-expression as well as for economic gain and spiritual growth.

This book investigates how a select group of contemporary santeros evaluate, reinvent, and represent santo making in New Mexico. I examine how certain Hispano artists negotiate the demands of a larger public to define their cultural identity and how others become models of cultural authenticity for their peers, protégés, and the dominant culture. In case studies of five artists whose wood carving is motivated primarily by one or two of the following factors—ethnic politics, the mainstream fine art world, tourism, or religion—I show how santeros manage tradition in a contemporary world. I focus a chapter each on Luis Tapia, an activist for ethnic awareness and a successful artist, savvy in the politics of the fine art world; on the late Patrocinio Barela, an art and cultural hero for early modernist artists and patrons and contemporary santeros; on Marco and Patricia Oviedo, prosperous art and tourism entrepreneurs and sophisticated packagers of tradition; and on the late Enrique Rendón, a devout santero who, in his lack of concern for defining tradition, became a model of cultural authenticity for other carvers and aficionados. Throughout my discussions of these carvers, I also address the related experiences of many other important contemporary santeros.

Many Hispano craftspeople, including Horacio Valdez, Orlando Romero, Marie Romero Cash, Luis Tapia, Félix López, and José Benjamín López, have incorporated the revivalism and the aesthetic preferences of the early Anglo artists and patrons into their work. They have successfully negotiated the economic and worldly forces of the revivalists and created their own expressions. Access to such empowerment is based on class and, to some extent, on gender. Most contemporary santeros are men, urban, and well educated.

All contemporary wood-carvers have sold santos and other carvings as art. Whether in their living rooms or at market booths, all contemporary santeros have been approached by Anglo patrons interested in acquiring their work. The buying and selling of Hispano religious images is now as essential as depicting the accurate iconography of individual saints. Contemporary wood-carvers recognize the power of the santo as commodity, and like their collectors, participate in patronage themselves.

In the past twenty years, exhibiting has been a primary means for artistic and cultural self-expression among Hispano artists. Exhibits, by way of Spanish Market displays, mainstream art museum shows, and private ethnic art collections "installed" in Anglo homes, are nothing new to native Hispanos. They have been the dominant culture's preferred means of presentation for as long as Anglos have come to New Mexico. Exhibits in their many forms represent power. Exhibit makers are in charge of selecting objects for display, and display has a direct effect: that santos are produced today is a result of their exhibition. Earlier in this century, exhibits, based on "outsider" aesthetics, took control from the local community. Today, contemporary wood-carvers work hard at maintaining a share of this control.

In the mainstream art world, the dominant culture's highest status is reserved for museum exhibitions, which use criteria centering on visual worthi-

Fig. 12. Collectors' display of santos in their Santa Fe home. From left to right: San Francisco de Asís (Saint Francis of Assisi), 1987, by Félix López; San Miguel Arcángel, 1991, by Luisito Luján; San Pedro Apóstol (Saint Peter the Apostle), 1991, by Frank Alarid. Courtesy Bud and Barbara Hoover. Photo: Mary Peck.

CRAFTING DEVOTIONS

ness in determining which objects to display. Fine art, therefore, has more value than ethnographic material culture. Western aesthetics take precedence over historical and cultural contexts.[7] Following this notion, early Anglo patrons and contemporary santeros alike have identified santos as art. Once devotions, the objects have become art. Although many santeros consider placement in any museum a heightening of value, particularly self-conscious artists feel they have "arrived" only when fine art museums display their work.

Early Anglo tradition seekers, such as Mabel Dodge Luhan and Frank Applegate, collected Spanish colonial santos for themselves, shifting the objects' meaning. By removing santos from churches and the homes of local parishioners, early collectors stripped the Spanish colonial images of their devotional use. Housing them in their living rooms, the new owners adopted colonial santos as foundlings and redefined them as antiques. The carvings became objects from a distant past that once had functional value to a certain community but that now had aesthetic and, perhaps, symbolic import for a culturally removed group of admirers. Like Hispanos, new Anglo owners revered their santos, but more for age, beauty, a vague notion of authenticity, and even a generalized spirituality than for religion.

Once they began collecting Spanish colonial santos, Anglo patrons donated some of their acquisitions to museums. In 1935, Alice Bemis Taylor gave Frank Applegate's santo collection to the new anthropology museum of the Colorado Springs Fine Arts Center, now the Taylor Museum.[8] In 1951, modernist painter Cady Wells donated his large collection of eighteenth- and nineteenth-century santos to the Museum of New Mexico. They are currently stored and displayed in the Museum of International Folk Art. These two gifts laid the groundwork for the two most significant museum collections of New Mexico religious folk art in this country. But not until the 1970s, when ethnically aware santeros developed their own painting styles, demonstrating that contemporary santos are more than just the product of revivalism, did most museums begin to acquire twentieth-century carvings. Generally, museum professionals considered revival items deriving from the 1920s less aesthetically, historically, or economically valuable than colonial images. For a long time, twentieth-century carvings remained in the public markets and the tourist shops.

Although most contemporary santeros are unschooled in art, some claim master Western sculptors and painters as their sources of inspiration. They produce abstract and figurative unpainted carvings as well as polychrome santos and refer to artists such as Constantin Brancusi, Henry Moore, and Pablo Picasso as their models. Brancusi and Moore were modernist sculptors hailed by other modernists for their reliance on non-Western art forms. Brancusi, Moore, and Picasso worked during the post–World War I era, when the Euro-American art world embraced the indigenous arts of Africa, Oceania, and the Americas, assigning them the problematic term *primitive,* which has evolutionist connotations.[9] During this time, Patrocinio Barela of Taos, a wood-carver who created figurative sculpture in juniper that to Western-trained eyes resembled other "primitive" forms, also gained stature in the fine art establishment.

Although ridiculed by members of his own community when he carved, Barela has become a model for contemporary carvers, including José Benjamín López, Félix López, Horacio Valdez, and his own grandson, Luis Barela, Jr. His appeal lies not only in that the mainstream art world hailed him, but that in his figurative and abstract sculpture, he produced a type of artwork other than santos.

Fig. 13. Wood carving by Patrocinio Barela, n.d. Collection: Dr. and Mrs. J. O. Domínguez. Photo: Mary Peck.

For contemporary carvers, Barela represents a daring sort of cultural creativity, whereby patrons and other outsiders had to accept the man's ingenuity on its own terms.

Contemporary carvers view their abstract sculpture as an opportunity to express themselves individually and as freedom from the constraints of tradition imposed on them by Anglo scholars, museum personnel, and consumers. Generally, carvers of abstract sculpture avoid Spanish Market; they do not like to be pigeonholed by outsiders as exemplars of a particular form, style, or historical perspective.

Some carvers, such as the Oviedos, Nicolás Herrera, and Félix López, reproduce the "museumizing" techniques of the dominant culture. They build adobe extensions onto their homes and workshops or restore existing historic structures. But they furnish these rooms with pedestals, track lighting, and, in some cases, didactic text, such as newspaper articles and identification labels next to objects on display.[10] They repeat the Anglo mode of juxtaposing modern conveniences and "old-style" ways of living and in the process replace the devotional aspect of santos with a quality of enshrinement associated more with putting objects under glass than with religion or outdoor craft fairs.

Along with individual wood-carvers, local retail establishments in northern New Mexico have patterned themselves on museums. The village of Chimayó, for example, has become aware of itself as a tourist attraction. Chimayó retailers and craftspeople constantly refine their presentations, establishing galleries as distinct from shops, improving on old store spaces by creating new, dramatic displays, and even, in religious contexts, protecting, and thereby identifying as valuable, certain artifacts by putting them behind glass.

Today, if santeros do not compete in the marketplace, their craft will not survive. In contemporary New Mexico, handmade santos still have a place in churches, but they are only one of many kinds of images available for use there. They compete with mass-produced plaster-of-Paris saints, lead statues, and chromolithographs. Alternatively, galleries, public markets, and museums provide exclusive showcases for "good quality" wood carvings. In fact, the presence of handmade santos in any setting creates a showcase atmosphere. Even on the altars of churches, handmade santos lend a "museumlike" quality to the religious institution. Along with the believers, leisure travelers visit churches to see Spanish colonial or contemporary Hispano art in a ritual setting. In this way, the church becomes a diorama for tourists, a representation of religion rather than an actual house of worship. Ultimately, it serves as another form of marketing.[11]

Some carvers, such the Oviedos, Sabinita López Ortiz, and Gloria López Córdova, who market their works from home, also show their work at Spanish Market. These artists do not necessarily view the Anglo-controlled public market and the private home as two competing sales outlets. Rather, they recognize and value the commercial benefits that participation in public markets may offer, and they view marketing their works from home as another opportunity to reap cash rewards. For some carvers, selling santos from home also offers an opportunity to improve on santos and therefore to increase the objects' economic power.

Along with relying on Anglo marketing techniques as a means to financial and cultural independence, contemporary santeros appropriate dominant culture roles. In the 1970s, in an attempt to achieve artistic freedom from Anglo control, santeros became their own curators. Luis Tapia, José Benjamín López,

Fig. 14. Interior, home of Nicolás Herrera, El Rito, 1992. Herrera has recently renovated and reinhabited this old adobe structure, located next to the frame house where he was raised, turning it into a place where he can display his large collection of antiques as well as his santos and retablos. He built a workshop on the second floor for making santos. Photo: Mary Peck.

<small>OVERLEAF</small>

Fig. 15. Detail of Nicolás Herrera's retablo display in his home and studio, El Rito, 1992. The Winter Spanish Market poster shows a reproduction of a retablo by Adam Alire, Herrera's teenage nephew who apprentices with his uncle. At the 1991 Winter Spanish Market, Alire won a ribbon for santos in the children's section. Photo: Mary Peck.

and others organized shows in local venues, mostly churches, selecting their own artworks and those of their friends for display. To locate what they considered traditional artwork, activist wood-carvers did research among *los viejos* (the old people) from the northern villages. Interviewing them to learn about the everyday life of their past, the santeros acted as field workers. Their agenda—to discover their own ethnicity and identity—was itself an early-twentieth-century Anglo notion, manifested by efforts to collect, revive, and market the local native crafts and other expressions of native life. For these carvers, as for the Anglo artists and patrons before them, the finding, or the discovery, of tradition was a means of discovering themselves. Because the means for self-discovery came, at least partially, from the dominant culture, I wonder whether the contemporary carvers made their efforts at self-identity in the Anglos' own pastoral image.

The showcase atmosphere associated with the presentation of santos not only manifests itself in the church, the museum, and the market, but also appears in tourism and entertainment. Contemporary santeros make hand-carved santos for the benefit of recreational travelers. Often stripped of their Hispano-Catholic attributes, by abandoning polychrome or creating images from the Old Testament, for example, contemporary santos have become collectible for the fun of it. Busloads of tourists travel the well-worn highways between Santa Fe and Taos, stopping at the homes of carvers, sometimes beckoned by signs. In their homes and workshops, carvers treat visitors to much more than attractive santos. They offer a hospitable climate and a glimpse of their everyday life. Some santeros build entire rooms for visitors, using local materials such as mud and straw. In season, they might offer visitors fruits or chili from the local harvest. Carvers also might introduce their family to tourists or invite visitors to sign a guest book. They provide a happy, even festive, spectacle that allows all to achieve perfect synchrony—everyone is on holiday, or so it seems. Folklorist Barbara Kirshenblatt-Gimblett's notion of "the life world of others as our playground" is borne out by some tour companies, who even visit the carvers' homes before they bring their travelers, checking that the guests will feel comfortable and safe.[12]

The iconographic and devotional value of santos is not, generally speaking, culturally portable beyond the Hispano-Catholic community. Contemporary carvers who have found a religious voice outside of their ethnic group are cultural negotiators. Charles Carrillo of Santa Fe, for example, an urban Ph.D. candidate in anthropology, integrated himself into the northern New Mexico rural community and now presents his discovery of tradition to the dominant culture. A member of the oldest practicing penitential brotherhood in New Mexico, Carrillo is also a descendant of one of New Mexico's earliest Hispano families. The religious devotion he discovered in himself as a scholar as well as a Hispano inspired him to carve. A citizen of multiple worlds, Carrillo struggles for an association between his craft and his religion. Increasingly, sales of his carvings help support his family.

Carrillo and other brothers who carve, such as Nicolás Herrera, sell their works primarily to folk-art collectors and museum professionals who dis-

Fig. 16. Marco Oviedo handing a business card to a potential patron at the 1991 Spanish Market. Photo: Miguel A. Gandert.

Fig. 17. Sabinita López Ortíz (far right) and
family in front of her wood-carving shop,
Córdova, 1991. Sitting directly behind Ortíz is
her uncle, George López, a famous carver who
taught her the craft. Photo: Mary Peck.

play them either as art or as representations of sacred belief and practice. These consumers usually have no personal religious affiliation with the objects. Without such patrons, however, Carrillo's and Herrera's works would have no reason to exist. Their santos would have no public audience. Most brothers in penitential chapters have little interest in contemporary handmade saints. For Carrillo and Herrera, the museum, the market, and the living room are currently the sole means available to them for presenting an artistic, religious expression. To a certain extent, they must craft tradition according to their patrons' expectations.

Certain carvers distinguish between different types of patrons and travelers. Some visitors take genuine interest in the region and have some knowledge and perhaps cash to make substantial purchases. Others have little knowledge of wood carving and less money. The carvers base this distinction on class. By way of education, some carvers have more in common with the patrons they favor than with other carvers. Educated carvers, such as Victor Goler and Marco and Patricia Oviedo, are often self-conscious about the art they make and have more affinity with the fine art world than with religion or popular culture. On the other hand, carvers with less education, such as Enrique Rendón and George López, were less self-conscious about their santos, associating them more with marketing and popular culture than with fine art. Rendón and López were devout Catholics, but unlike their educated and more urban colleagues, such as Carrillo and Luis Tapia, they viewed their carvings as something other than sacred. The santos they actually used in prayer were often mass-produced or historic. In spite of such differences based on class, differences between educated and noneducated wood-carvers are specific and always in flux.

Fig. 18. Interior of Sabinita Ortíz's wood-carving shop, Córdova, 1991. A framed photograph on the wall above the carvings shows early-twentieth-century wood-carver and entrepreneur, José Dolores López, and his family. José Dolores was George López's father. Photo: Mary Peck.

Fig. 19. Advertising signs, Chimayó, 1991.
Photo: Mary Peck.

Fig. 20. Charles M. Carrillo with prize-winning
bulto of Nuestra Señora de los Dolores, E. Boyd
Memorial Award, 1991 Spanish Market. On each
of the seven swords piercing this grieving Virgin's
heart, Carrillo painted the seven sorrows. They
are: the Flight into Egypt, the Circumcision, el
Niño Perdido (the Lost Christ Child), la Via Crucis
(the Way of the Cross, or Christ Carrying the
Cross), the Crucifixion, Descent from the Cross,
and the Entombment. Photo: Miguel A. Gandert.

Fig. 21. Nicolás Herrera with life-sized Carretta
de la Muerte, 1991 Spanish Market.
Thumbtacked to the carretta are Herrera's
laminated description of the image's religious
meaning and my business card indicating that
the museum purchased the object. Collection:
Gene Autry Western Heritage Museum. Photo:
Miguel A. Gandert.

< **Fig. 22.** Bulto of Sacred Heart of Jesus, 1986, by
Enrique Rendón, cottonwood, pine, rocks, paint.
Collection: Gene Autry Western Heritage
Museum. Gift of Robert and Ruth Vogele. Photo:
Susan Einstein.

Fig. 23. Trade sign for Córdova wood-carving
establishment of George López and Lawrence
Ortíz. Sabinita Ortíz removed this sign from the
front of her house and her Uncle George's home
in 1991, replacing it with two new versions.
Instead of listing Lawrence Ortíz along with
George López, each new sign has included
Sabinita's name as a wood-carver. Lawrence
Ortíz, Sabinita's husband, has never made wood
carvings. Collection: Gene Autry Western
Heritage Museum. Gift of Sabinita López Ortíz.
Photo: Susan Einstein.

Fig. 24. Gloria López Córdova in her workshop, Córdova, 1991. Photo: Mary Peck.

In recent years, Hispano women have taken a more assertive role in carving images. Although there are no records of women carving saints in the colonial period, throughout the twentieth century women have participated in men's woodcarving along with creating their own one-person industries.[13] Women sometimes paint their husbands' carvings or collect local materials for making natural pigments. They assist in setting up booths at public markets and with bookkeeping. Gloria López Córdova, Marie Romero Cash, and Marie's sister, Anita Romero Jones, are carvers who have achieved an independent expressive voice within the carving industry. Córdova, who began carving under the signature of a male relative, has become recognized for her mastery of decorative skill. Through her independent research, Cash has become an authority for other carvers, scholars, and laypeople on the construction, attributes, and history of Spanish colonial santos. Cash and Jones have signed their own works since they began carving. Within the past decade, all the women who participate in the craft, including those who collaborate with their husbands, such as Zoraida Ortega and Patricia Oviedo, have begun signing the bottoms of their carvings. The contemporary recognition of women's roles in making saints is another example of how the politics of self-expression are constantly renegotiated in santo production.

Individual artists tend to work primarily within one or two of the frameworks of ethnic politics, connoisseurship, tourism, or religion; however, their carving repertoires suggest interaction with multiple worlds. For example, Luis Tapia positions himself within the contexts of ethnic awareness and the fine art world, but he has also installed a large altar screen in a church where he has worshipped. Others, such as Enrique Rendón, have crafted carvings in a style that caters to the desires of leisure travelers yet rejected the opportunity to participate in public craft fairs organized by Anglo professionals. In the late twentieth century, the expressive possibilities for northern New Mexico wood-carvers are dynamic and complex; the expression itself is open for constant reinvention.

Carvers differ in their attitudes to the multiple meanings of santos and their settings. For example, Marco and Patricia Oviedo and Luis Tapia have all won prizes for their santos at Spanish Market, but the Oviedos take great pride in their awards and display the ribbons they receive for the benefit of patrons. Luis Tapia appreciates such honors, too, but he has more concern for the way he directs the style of his work than for how judges assess it. He has misplaced his award ribbons completely. Marco and Patricia Oviedo and Luis Tapia all use sophisticated methods for merchandising their carvings to connoisseurs and other art collectors, but the Oviedos establish very complex systems for accepting commissions, whereas Tapia sells his work through an elite gallery that discourages such requests. Hispano carvers who have not been born into native New Mexican families, such as Marco Oviedo and Victor Goler, try very hard to assert their rightful place as local santeros. Others, such as Patrocinio Barela, who also was not New Mexican by birth, pursued carving, caring not at all about lineage.

In spite of the wood-carvers' various attitudes toward the market and tradition, the value system of the dominant culture is the measuring stick against which they all gauge their work. Contemporary makers of handmade santos and other wood carvings either approve of public markets sponsored by Anglos or they don't. They either contribute to mainstream museum shows or they mount their own grass-roots exhibitions separate from but in the same presentational mode as dominant institutions. Some carvers, particularly the well-educated, replicate museum displays in their homes. Others, with less exposure to such elite cultural institutions, nevertheless construct showcase environments for the exclusive benefit of patrons. All contemporary santeros negotiate dominant aesthetic and anthropological categories and means of presentation for their own use.

Although using Anglo models to achieve expressive independence may at first seem contradictory, this book explores the way carvers must address these incongruities in order to achieve cultural and individual power. In focusing on Luis Tapia's ethnic politics and artistic successes, Patrocinio Barela's celebrity among Anglos and Hispanos, Marco and Patricia Oviedos' creative commodification of heritage, and Enrique Rendón's pure delight in the nature of carving, I will address certain questions: Who has the power? How do the wood-carvers legitimize their notions of tradition? Does the opportunity to exhibit put someone in charge? With whom are the carvers in competition for control—art dealers? museum professionals? other villagers? other wood-carvers?

I raise these questions to direct attention to the diversity of relationships between carvers and their saints. I also intend to show how such a contemporary craft can only prosper in a tangled web of political, aesthetic, commercial, and religious forces. In turn, this tangle leads to complicated cultural negotiations and representations. For today's New Mexico santeros, this complexity is a means to cultural authenticity.

1

CHICANO ART
AND SANTOS
BY LUIS TAPIA

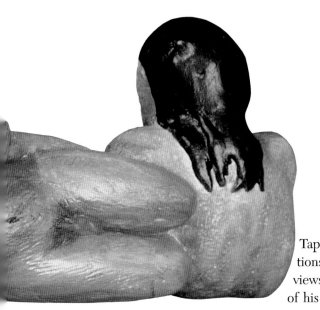

La Cruz de Animas (The Cross of the Souls),
1993, by Luis Tapia. Detail of fig. 43.

LUIS TAPIA IS ONE OF THE LEADING SANTEROS to have emerged in the last twenty years. After years of political and artistic struggle, Tapia is now famous. He exhibits his wood carvings in major fine art exhibitions and sells them to important museums throughout the country. In interviews he speaks not only of his experience with his culture and his art but also of his interactions with patrons, curators, and scholars. Luis Tapia negotiates personal research of Hispano traditions, ethnic pride, the values of the dominant culture, and a need for an individual style with a larger goal of being a successful artist. Tapia is a "fine-art santero," selling his work through an exclusive gallery, but still, he makes constant reference to identity and tradition. He participates in a variety of worlds.

Tapia's santo production mirrors the historic progression of the national Chicano movement, or El Movimiento, which surfaced in the mid-1960s as a mass political project and continues in the present as a platform of cultural negotiation for Hispano artists and activists.[1] In the mid-1970s, dissatisfied with the way the dominant culture treated him, Luis Tapia set out to discover his own ethnic identity. With his now former wife, Star, his cousin, the painter Frederico Vigil, and others, Tapia conducted grass-roots field work among members of rural New Mexico Hispano communities. He was determined to define native culture for himself. Making santos, he recalls, was a direct result of this research.[2]

Throughout the 1970s, Tapia worked to gain recognition for northern New Mexico Hispano craftspeople, primarily through organizing La Cofradía de Artes y Artesanos Hispanicos (The Brotherhood of Hispano Arts and Artists), a local nonprofit association. Tapia and his friends wanted to express ethnicity,

artistic freedom, and freedom from Anglo-American control.[3] Along the way, Tapia achieved critical acclaim for his work. In 1976 and 1977, he and Star accepted invitations to participate in the Smithsonian Institution's Festival of American Folklife, and Tapia won blue ribbons for the polychrome santos he was among the first to introduce into the Santa Fe Spanish Market.[4] With this recognition, Tapia worked even harder to develop a unique aesthetic style.

Since the mid-1980s, curators, collectors, and art dealers have ushered Luis Tapia's santos into the fine-art world under the guise of sculpture. Owings-Dewey Fine Art in Santa Fe, a gallery frequented by cosmopolitan patrons, is the exclusive dealer for Tapia's carvings. In 1986, the Houston Fine Arts Center blockbuster traveling exhibition "Hispanic Art in the United States: Thirty Contemporary Painters and Sculptors" included Tapia's work.

Tapia's santos are iconographically correct, and many have found sacred homes in churches. But it is the opportunity to express himself individually and honestly more than the pious quality or indigenous materials of the saints that inspire his carving. Still, according to Tapia, the "art part" of making saints, like mixing natural pigments or religious devotion, is also traditional. Aesthetic concerns as well as functional needs were important to earlier artists as well.

An urban santero with an agenda both political and artistic, Luis Tapia mythologizes tradition. He carefully selects elements from the past that reinforce the ideology underlying his wood carvings. This chapter, about Luis Tapia's carvings, places the artist's art within the framework of the Chicano movement and shows how politics can support a New Mexico wood-carver's manipulation and invention of cultural identity. By charting the shift in tensions inherent in

Fig. 25. Luis Tapia in his studio, 1991. Tapia's son, Sergio, is in the back of the studio, painting a santo. Photo: Miguel A. Gandert.

Opposite

Fig. 26. Bulto of San Miguel Arcángel, ca. 1970s, by Luis Tapia. Collection: Spanish Colonial Arts Society, Inc. Collection on loan to the Museum of New Mexico, Museum of International Folk Art, Santa Fe. Photo: Blair Clark.

Tapia's relationship with the mainstream art world, I demonstrate how his desire to uphold and understand what he defines as tradition is also an appropriation and construction of it.

BEGINNINGS

Luis Tapia was born in 1950 in the village of Agua Fría, New Mexico, a small, rural Hispano community just west of urban Santa Fe. Although it maintains a strong Hispano community and an associated reputation as a poor and dangerous place, increasing numbers of Anglos have been moving there. According to one native Texan who recently purchased a home in Agua Fría, it represents a "real" community, where everyday people live, unlike the wealthy, outsider population that lives in Santa Fe.

Tapia's father, Benny, died when Luis was an infant. His mother, Pauline, raised him and his brother, Ben, alone. After graduating from St. Michael's High School, a parochial school in Santa Fe, Tapia enrolled at New Mexico State University in Las Cruces. A year later, his unruly and rebellious behavior caused his expulsion. Reminiscing about his student experience, Tapia recalls that a few years after the university required him to leave, it graciously invited him back—this time to give demonstrations of his wood carving. Tapia had no value to the school as an unruly mainstream student, but as an unschooled ethnic artist, he became desirable.

From the beginning of his full-time woodworking career, in 1972, Tapia integrated his work and family life. He left his job as manager of Cooper's Western Wear to work at home, where he could spend time with his family. He taught his son Sergio how to make santos almost as soon as he established himself as a carver. Star also produced Hispano crafts. Where her husband favored santos, Star preferred the ornamental straw work, or "poor man's gilding," of the eighteenth and nineteenth centuries.[5] This is a craft in which people cut wheat and oak stalks and corn husks into tiny pieces and apply them in intricate geometric designs to dark wood. Ornamental straw work often appeared on small crosses, candle sconces, *nichos* (small tabernacles), frames for religious statues and paintings, and trinket boxes.[6]

Although folk artists traditionally acquire their skills from older family members or other master craftspeople, Luis and Star taught themselves. They selected the Spanish colonial art form they felt best suited them. Both consider their work as the perpetuation of tradition.

RESISTANCE

Although the Tapias are self-taught, they learned about their crafts through associations they made with members of rural communities along the Rio Grande. In the early 1970s, the Tapias and Frederico Vigil traveled north from Santa Fe to interview *los viejitos* (the old people) about what Tapia calls "the rich blood of our history."[7] Like other ethnic activists of the late 1960s and early 1970s, Tapia, his family, and his local Hispano friends tired of the way their cultures and their lives had been invented by others. They turned to the four-hundred-year-old presence of Spanish culture in New Mexico, treating it as a source of pride. And they banded together to take hold of their own identities. Finding local artists

Fig. 27. Large processional cross, 1991, by Jimmy E. Trujillo, wood, paint, straw inlay, varnish, 63" x 10 1/2". Blue ribbon for other media, 1991 Spanish Market. Collection: Gene Autry Western Heritage Museum. Photo: Susan Einstein.

Fig. 28 *Cristo Crucificado* (Christ Crucified),
1989, by Luisito Luján, aspen, pine, paint, straw
inlay, varnish. Collection: Gene Autry Western
Heritage Museum. Photo: Susan Einstein.

Fig. 29. Adobe chapel built by members of Po
Ae Pi, ca. 1984, Santa Fe. Door by Wilberto
Miera. Established in Santa Fe in the early 1980s,
Po Ae Pi was a short-lived organization of
Hispano and Indian artists dedicated to artistic
and cultural freedom. Courtesy Dr. E. B. Hall.
Photo: Mary Peck.

who produced handmade items similar to those of the Spanish colonial era, primarily religious objects, and within a prevailing Chicano political ideal of preserving the culture of the rural agrarian class, Tapia and his friends claimed the local crafts as their own heritage.[8]

Tapia made little distinction between his urban background in and near Santa Fe and that of the rural, secluded villagers he interviewed and worked with. Instead, he and his friends did what many Chicano activists around the nation did at the time. Ignoring class differences, they focused on a shared ethnic background. Ultimately they constructed a Hispano cultural identity that reflected their cultural politics.

Eventually, the Tapias and Vigil organized the local artists into La Cofradía de Artes y Artesanos Hispanicos. The purpose of this group was "to encourage the revival, continuation, and growth of traditional and contemporary Hispano arts and crafts."[9] The term *cofradía* applies to a wide range of Catholic lay organizations. In northern New Mexico, the most familiar is La Cofradía de Nuestro Padre Jesús Nazareno (The Brotherhood of our Father Jesus the Nazarene), a widespread and vital organization that encourages penitential discipline. Historically, cofradías have represented a central and enduring symbol of Hispano identity, resistance to Anglo-American hegemony, and the different character of northern European Catholicism.

Tapia and his colleagues probably chose cofradía as their name because of its association with defiance and struggle. Without establishing any formal ties with El Movimiento, La Cofradía had an agenda that paralleled that of the national Chicano art movement. Developed outside the dominant museum, gallery, and arts-publication circuit, La Cofradía enabled Hispano artists to have their own voice in promoting their cultural heritage. Perhaps most significant is that it did not accept outside Anglo criteria that determined what was traditional and what was not. La Cofradía created grass-roots art exhibitions in local churches and community centers, and occasionally for museums. Friends of the artists and the artists themselves mounted the shows.

According to its founders, La Cofradía exhibitions accomplished two goals. First, they gave exposure to what Tapia and Vigil considered a large coterie of undiscovered New Mexican artists making objects based in Hispano traditions, and second, they showed the public that Hispanos were capable of organizing themselves as well as exhibitions of their art. The shows included works ranging from santos to woven textiles to furniture and tinwork, representing art forms produced in the colonial period. But they also showcased a variety of stylistic, thematic, and decorative innovations that the artists had incorporated into older forms. The criteria for selecting works for the cofradía exhibitions were far less rigid than those, say, for the Spanish Market. However, the exhibition and market format for displaying the works, or more poignantly, the fact of displaying the works at all, was identical to the dominant culture's means of presentation.

From the beginning, Tapia was not content merely to replicate the styles and forms of his forebears. In keeping with the Chicano movement, he wanted more than just to reclaim vernacular traditions. Rather, Tapia worked to reinterpret traditions in ways useful to his political, social, and cultural experience.[10] He incorporated what he considered to be modern influences into his wood carvings and promoted the new styles of other Hispano artists. In the late 1970s, Tapia argued, "[Anglo judges and promoters] tell us to stick with the techniques

Fig. 30. Interior, Po Ae Pi chapel. Top row (left to right): Cristo, 1984, by Charles M. Carrillo, after the Cristo in El Santuario de Chimayó, oil on canvas; altar painting, 1985, by Monica Roybal; altar panels, 1984, by Monica Roybal; bultos of Santa Clara de Asís (Saint Claire of Assisi), Santo Niño de Atocha (the Holy Child of Atocha), and San Francisco de Asís, n.d., unidentified; retablo of Holy Trinity, 1985, by Marie Romero Cash, tin frame by Don Cash. Middle right: retablo of the Flight from Egypt, n.d., unidentified. Bottom: painting, 1984, by Frederico Vigil; retablo of Devociónes de Nuevo Mexico (New Mexico Devotions), 1985, by Charles M. Carrillo. Courtesy Dr. E. B. Hall. Photo: Mary Peck.

of 200 years ago, but there's a lot of people working today with a whole lot of modern influences that are worth appreciating."[11]

In the mid-1970s, modern interpretations of Spanish colonial art consisted mainly of the introduction of painted santos into the Spanish Market. Polychromed images had not been produced since the late nineteenth century, when wood-carvers made images for use exclusively by members of their own communities. Ironically, the innovative painted santos of the contemporary period look just like the older traditional images.

Before the arrival of painted santos in the early 1970s, the Spanish Market had a lot of what Tapia referred to as "the Córdovas,...the Ben Ortegas,...santos [by local carvers that] weren't painted." Left unpainted and chip-carved, or incised, these did not resemble colonial santos at all, although they appeared in a market that from the beginning prided itself on preserving tradition.[12] The Spanish Colonial Arts Society equated colonial and traditional; however, they limited the production of "traditional" items in favor of such contemporary popular forms as lazy susans, record racks, and magnets.[13] Anglo tastes also influenced the decoration of many of these objects, and this meant that pieces were often left unpainted.

With their painted santos, Tapia and other carvers, such as Orlando Romero and Horacio Valdez, challenged the twentieth-century canon of Spanish colonial–style art. Whereas in the mid-1970s the society's traditional mandate reflected an Anglo-dominated construction of purity and authenticity, the contemporary santos by Luis Tapia and others looked old but represented empowerment and change. Although the ideological constructs of the contempo-

Fig. 31. Ben Ortega's Spanish Market display of his carvings, 1990. Photo: Miguel A. Gandert.

CRAFTING DEVOTIONS

rary wood-carvers and the Spanish Colonial Arts Society resembled each other—to revive the handmade material culture of the Spanish colonial era—the groups' redefinitions of tradition were at odds.

Ultimately, the differences between the traditional canon of the SCAS and Luis Tapia's innovative artistic goals became too great, and Tapia stopped participating. Still, for the duration of Tapia's tenure in the market, from the mid-1970s to the early 1980s, he and the market benefited. When he first showed his work at the market in 1974, Tapia "took first, second, and third in the [santo division]." The following year "[SCAS curator] Alan Vedder got [Tapia] to do furniture. And that was the first time that [the market] ever had furniture." Since then, furniture making has become an integral part of Tapia's woodworking.

After leaving the Spanish Market, Tapia turned to La Cofradía de Artes y Artesanos Hispanicos as an alternative means of expressing himself. Along with his cousin Vigil, he curated a number of his own exhibitions of Hispano New Mexican crafts, mounting them in local churches and museums that would agree to have the shows on the curators' terms.

After a few years of administering La Cofradía and planning its exhibitions, Tapia and Vigil found that they had too little time for their own artwork. At the same time, personal struggles affected the cohesion of the organization. Although Tapia and Vigil maintained a firm belief in the original purpose of La Cofradía, "to encourage the revival, continuation, and growth of traditional and contemporary Hispano arts and crafts," they both decided to give priority to their individual artistic careers. Unable to find anyone to replace them as chair and vice-chair, Tapia, Vigil, and other board members officially disbanded La Cofradía de Artes y Artesanos Hispanicos in 1983.

STYLE AND INVENTION

Although his family did not encourage him at the beginning, Luis Tapia continued his woodworking and excelled in a variety of ways. Although more santeros rely on their carving to make a living today than a decade ago, Tapia is unusual because from the beginning of his career he devoted himself entirely to his art. Until the early 1990s, he supported himself primarily by making furniture. Tapia also carved and painted santos, but he could not rely on their sales until Owings-Dewey Fine Art began to sell every santo he made. At first, Tapia made reproduction furniture and traditional-style santos, copying earlier Spanish colonial pieces. Later, he "began developing his own style" by allowing himself more freedom in his decorative techniques, forms, and subject matter.[14]

Style has always been important to Tapia. According to Félix López, another renowned carver, Tapia's work is distinctive because of its novelty. His most recent santo and furniture innovations are evident in his polychrome decoration. Color is important to Tapia, and he has always used acrylic paints, achieving bright surfaces. He claims that underneath the yellowed varnish of Spanish colonial santos, the original colors were radiant.[15] Tapia considers the application of color on his saints and other carvings as traditional, but he also employs it for originality. His luminous greens, reds, blues, and yellows look equally well on images of saints, a *cholo* couple, and tourists. The bright colors Tapia chooses make his subjects appear contemporary, not antique.

Tapia's experimental use of paint makes the wood-carving tradition live in other ways. Recently, on the table of a reredos and on the base of an image of

OVERLEAF

Left

Fig. 32. *José y María*, 1991, by Luis Tapia. Collection: Barbara Windom and Victor DiSuvero. Courtesy Owings-Dewey Fine Art.

Right

Fig. 33. *Folk Art Collectors,* 1992, by Luis Tapia. Collection: Lynn Steuer. Courtesy Owings-Dewey Fine Art.

San José, Tapia painted the surfaces to simulate the grain of wood underneath. Another image, a brightly painted San Pedro, stands on a wooden base painted to look like a brick surface and holds the keys to a Spanish colonial–style door behind him.

Like the colonial *carpinteros* (carpenters) before him, Tapia also applies color to his furniture. He often uses the same red and green shades that were common in eighteenth- and nineteenth-century furniture.[16] But he is not merely content to reintroduce the styles of the colonial *carpinteros* into his contemporary furniture; Tapia recalls other historical precedents to decorate his pieces. He combines various designs and techniques in a richly nuanced interchange; this is his aesthetic strategy.[17]

Like the colonial santeros, who decorated the reredos and walls of village churches, Tapia paints the illusion of architectural relief onto his furniture. On a *trastero* he produced in 1989, for example, he painted six columns that frame the front door panels. Although columns like these were not common on colonial *trasteros,* they do appear as flat painted images or sculpture on altar screens. Tapia also painted an image of turned splats, or thin pieces of wood, on the front panels of this piece. Historically, the front doors of many colonial *trasteros* were made of turned splats rather than panels.[18]

Tapia's recent use of color on furniture is more personally and aesthetically motivated than political. Unlike his mid-1970s Spanish Market exhibits, which involved other santeros and were thus collective, Tapia's current painting is more of an individual endeavor. His rationale for adding color to his furniture is similar to his earlier argument for painting santos—that underneath dark coats of varnish, bright colors were used on colonial furniture.[19] However, the work's artistic merit now outshines its symbolic connection to ethnic pride. In 1988, a National Public Radio interviewer asked about the color he used on a set of polychromed chairs. Tapia mused, "It's actually a painting, in a way."[20]

The aesthetic value Tapia now attaches to his work is historically situated. Fifteen years elapsed between his introducing painted santos to the Spanish Market and his sweeping entrance into the fine-art world, where his santos and furniture are available exclusively through Owings-Dewey Fine Art. Tapia's carvings, originally objects of cultural import, became pieces of "art." This transformation reflects a national trend in the Chicano movement, in which artists who once made art out of a political need now participate in the world of fine-art negotiations. It also reflects a contemporary development among curators, art dealers, collectors, and others who reposition folk art, certain antiques, and outsider art into the mainstream, elevating their status through the art establishment.[21]

APPROPRIATIONS

In his furniture making, Tapia revels in the exploration of his own style. It also earns him a solid living. Since the late 1970s, Tapia has worked on contract for the Museum of International Folk Art in Santa Fe and for various Santa Fe art galleries, restoring and preserving Spanish colonial furniture. Although he views his contractual work as something that simply allows him to pay the bills, it nonetheless has ties to his efforts on behalf of cultural awareness. Tapia has become an expert in historic furniture and its conservation because of Anglo curator

Fig. 34. Reredos, 1990, by Luis Tapia, wood, tin, plastic flowers, bright acrylic paint. At the base of this altar screen, along with his signature, Tapia wrote, "Dedico este altar a la memoria de mi amigo Chris Corriz 1974/1990" (I dedicate this altar to the memory of my friend Chris Corriz 1974–1990). Corriz, also a friend of Tapia's son, assisted in the building of this altar and died a few days before it was completed. Collection: Gene Autry Western Heritage Museum. Photo: Susan Einstein.

OVERLEAF

Left

Fig. 35. *San Pedro Apóstol*, 1991, by Luis Tapia. Collection: Enid and Gary Freund. Courtesy Owings-Dewey Fine Art.

Right

Fig. 36. Trastero, 1989, by Luis Tapia. Collection: The Heard Museum. Photo: Craig Smith.

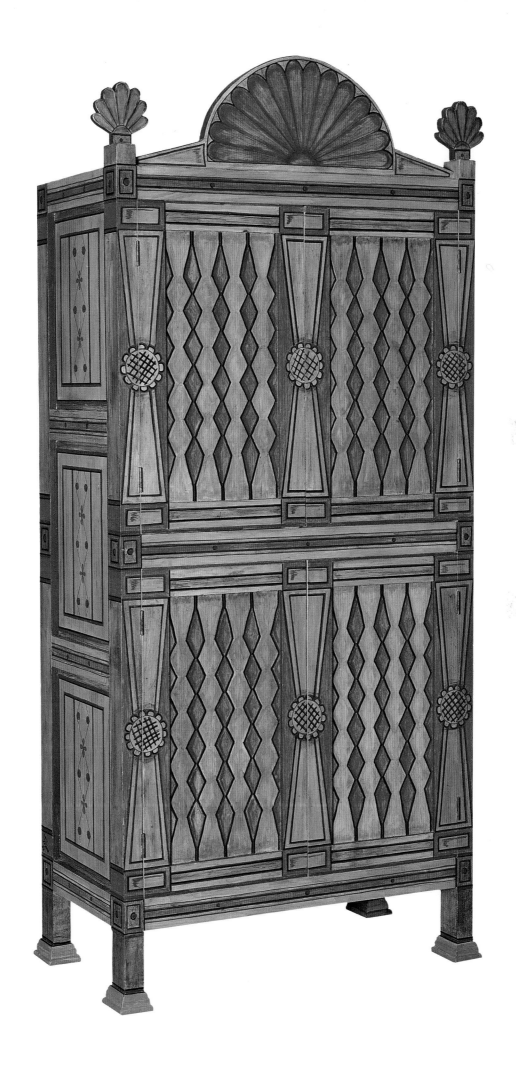

Alan Vedder's encouragement, his own research in museum collections, and a general exposure to Spanish colonial material culture. He has assumed cultural responsibility for producing Spanish colonial–style furniture, and he has even passed on his skills to his son Sergio.

Most, if not all, of Tapia's restoration and preservation work comes from Anglo clients. A native craftsperson hired by members of the dominant culture, Tapia is acutely self-conscious about the politics of preservation. He acknowledges that curators and conservators have a preference for preservation, the stabilization or repair of an artifact to prevent further damage, over restoration, bringing an object back to its former condition, and he has formed opinions about this difference. Tapia also struggles with issues of cultural appropriation, special interest groups taking custody of particular cultural expressions, which are implicit in the preservationist enterprise.

In 1988, questions I asked Tapia about the early-twentieth-century Hispano wood-carvers led to the subject of preservation. Tapia owned a couple of pieces by Celso Gallegos, church sacristan from Agua Fría who, in the 1920s and 1930s, made stone and wood carvings based in religious and secular themes. When I remarked on the especially dark and shiny appearance of one wooden image by Gallegos of Saint Anthony, Tapia explained that he waxed the piece to prevent its deterioration. Perhaps sensing my curatorial concern over the owner's license to alter the appearance of art, Tapia validated his preservation efforts by arguing that wood-carvers of the early twentieth century also acted as self-taught preservationists. He mentioned Patrocinio Barela as an example of an innovative wood-carver who began his career by repairing colonial santos. Although Tapia's preservation method altered the work visually, the carver legitimized the process by "traditionalizing" it, by associating it with the practices of a renowned wood-carver.

Wilberto Miera, Luis Tapia's close friend, is another contemporary wood-carver who negotiates the politics of preservation and conservation in his work. In the late 1980s, Miera worked on the restoration of a house originally owned by early Santa Fe art colonists Gerald Cassidy and Ina Sizer Cassidy. The house is located on fashionable Canyon Road, on Santa Fe's largely Anglo east side. Working in the house, Miera replaced rotten vigas (wooden ceiling beams) and floor joists, and replastered walls the Spanish colonial way—with mud.

When Miera worked on the Cassidy house, a commercial design company called Southwest Spanish Craftsmen owned it. The company used it as their showroom for the Spanish colonial–style furniture and architectural crafts they sold. Working with Southwest Spanish Craftsmen enabled Miera to become particularly skilled at producing Spanish Colonial–style wooden doors. Hand-carved doors, like handmade furniture and santos, are emblematic of northern New Mexico Hispano culture. Just as Tapia began learning furniture making thanks to Alan Vedder, Miera's work for the largely Anglo firm helped him learn a craft that he now considers part of his inherited tradition. Miera also feels that his specialized commercial work gave him an opportunity to develop an individual style.

In the late 1980s, neither Luis Tapia nor Wilberto Miera were pleased with the restoration, preservation, or conservation work being done on local Spanish colonial art and architecture. To them, restoration, preservation, and conservation represented an elite power structure. Tapia and Miera made their position on this issue clear by using the example of the restoration of the historic

Fig. 37. Wilberto Miera in his studio, Santa Fe, 1992. Miera is making this cross as a cemetery marker. Photo: Mary Peck

Overleaf

Left

Fig. 38. Doors in Santa Fe home, n.d., by Wilberto Miera. Courtesy Ray and Judy Dewey. Photo: Mary Peck.

Right

Fig. 39. Reredos in San Ildefonso mission, ca. 1979, by Luis Tapia. Courtesy tribal authorities, San Ildefonso Pueblo, and Craft & Folk Art Museum, Los Angeles. Photo: Mary Peck.

church of Our Lady of Guadalupe in Santa Fe. A Chicago family who owned a second home in Santa Fe offered a gift of forty thousand dollars to refurbish the church, which badly needed repair. The family stipulated that the restoration involve community members. Because an outside contractor did the repairs on the church, and the building committee could not make a decision regarding what era the building should be restored to, the Chicago family took their money back. The work on the historic church remains unfinished. Tapia's opinion about the choice of restorer: "It's not a question of what's there: it's a question of their names. They [Anglos] don't really understand it." Miera echoed Tapia's frustration with the selection of a nonlocal and non-Hispanic restorer by saying that the church is "out of our control. . . . It's not even close to what it should be."

Tapia and Miera associate restoration, preservation, and conservation with Anglos. When they discuss ownership of Spanish colonial art, they also attribute power to the Anglos. For Tapia, preservation of art and architecture is connected to issues of home ownership in Santa Fe. He says, "The Anglos ended up with our [adobe homes] and we ended up with theirs [prefab, aluminum]. They're making money off of theirs and we're trying to sell ours and we can't." Once Hispano tradition gets into the hands of Anglo capitalists, it becomes a valuable commodity. Once Anglo popular culture reaches the hands of New Mexican Hispano communities, it diminishes in economic worth. A large gap develops between institutional preservationists and the bearers of tradition.

Still, although Tapia and Miera recognize the distinction between institutional preservationists and tradition bearers, they do not view the problem as insurmountable. According to Tapia, "[Hispanos have] exchanged all our products with the Anglos. . . . But I think it helps the [Hispano] culture grow."[22] What Tapia and Miera ask is not necessarily to be given back a culture or an adobe-style home, but rather to be included in the process of reevaluating and restoring the material expressions that they claim as theirs.

An altar screen he painted in the late 1970s is a fine example of Tapia's attitude toward preserving the past while making new art. The San Ildefonso church, which commissioned the work, is itself the result of revivalism and preservation efforts. Built in 1958, the present structure is the third on the site. The original was partially destroyed in a fire. Built by the renowned preservationist architect John Gaw Meem, the new San Ildefonso church reflects a revival of seventeenth-century building practice and design.[23] In keeping with the spirit of preservation surrounding the rebuilding of the church, the governor of San Ildefonso Pueblo commissioned Tapia to make an altar screen in the Spanish colonial style.

The artist's efforts at building the reredos for San Ildefonso Pueblo were masterful. Tapia relied on a variety of historical and some contemporary sources. He painted a Franciscan symbol on the bottom center panel of the altar with a protruding table above it supported by short twisted carved pillars that resemble baroque Salomonic pillars found in painted and carved form in various New Mexican mission churches.[24] He carved a portable wooden tabernacle, placing it on the altar table in the center of the reredos. Above the altar table he created five panels in two tiers; at the top are San Juan Nepomuceno and San José, common saints in the New Mexico pantheon. Below are two Indian saints, Juan Diego wearing a *mantilla* (shawl) depicting the Virgin of Guadalupe and Kateri Tekakwitha, a Mohawk saint and the first American Indian canonized by the Catholic church. In the center is a two-tiered panel of a painted niche with a

Cristo (Spanish colonial crucifix) hanging on top of it. According to Tapia, the santero Molleno, a prolific artist active in the first half of the nineteenth century, carved the Cristo, a representation of Esquípulas, named for the cult of the Christ of Esquípulas from Guatemala. Tapia framed all five panels with painted columns, and he painted half-diamond designs on all the horizontal borders of the altar screen. He carved the top finials of the screen in scallop motifs. On the crest he displayed a painted image of the Trinity, as well as pictures of the sun, the moon, and a rainbow.

The various historical sources Tapia used to make the altar screen at San Ildefonso Pueblo connect it to its contemporary space. Because the Cristo by Molleno is older than the new San Ildefonso church, Tapia links both the altar screen and its church to the earlier ecclesiastical building constructed on the Pueblo. Pioneering New Mexico Spanish colonial art historian E. Boyd identified three other images of Esquípulas located in nearby churches and her assertion that "the cult of the Christ of Esquípulas from Guatemala was not then limited to the shrine at the healing mud springs at Chimayó" links Tapia's altar screen to other communities that follow the cult of Esquípulas.[25] By including Indian motifs along with the image of the Trinity on the crest, Tapia recalls the painting on the interior of earlier mission churches, especially the one at Laguna Pueblo, where religious symbols are mixed. Tapia also acknowledges the syncretism that is part of native religions on almost all the Southwestern pueblos.

By introducing Indian saints onto the altar panels, particularly the Mohawk Kateri Tekakwitha, Tapia affirms a contemporary relationship between Hispano and Native American culture. This also marks an artistic innovation for Tapia. According to Tapia, contemporary santeros generally like to carve santos other than just those the colonial communities favored.[26] Tapia claims that he himself has done "a lot of research of saints that traditionally were not part of New Mexican folk art." The Anglo priesthood calls Kateri Tekakwitha, quite poignantly, the "the Lily of the Mohawks." Her tribal neighbors reportedly referred to her as "the fairest flower that ever bloomed among the redmen."[27] She was only presented as a candidate for sainthood in this century. Kateri Tekakwitha could not have been part of the pantheon of colonial New Mexican saints. By 1988, Tapia had made approximately eight images of Kateri, and he still had more ideas for making others.[28]

Tapia's altar screen incorporates the spirit of revivalism surrounding the John Gaw Meem church where it is housed. His artistic innovations demonstrate a sensitivity to the fact that this is a Spanish colonial–style altar within an Indian pueblo. But the governor elected at San Ildefonso Pueblo in 1989 ordered Tapia's reredos forcibly removed from the front of the church's nave. According to Tapia, the governor did not want the screen in the pueblo church because it was made by a Hispano. Tapia recalls that controversy over his ethnicity also surrounded the original commission to make the reredos; however, Father Conran, the parish priest at the time, specifically wanted him to make the screen, so he completed the job. Tapia found the removal of his reredos upsetting. Although moving it caused irreparable damage to the piece, he felt that it was not his place to try to save the screen. According to Tapia, the pueblo owned the piece: "If [the screen] doesn't survive, well, it went the way it's supposed to go." This echoes the artist's position on an altar screen he restored for the Ranchos de Taos mission. Tapia claimed that once he finished painting it, "that image is no longer mine. . . . The community defines it. It belongs to the community."[29]

Fig. 40. Laguna Pueblo Mission interior, ca. 1940. Courtesy Museum of New Mexico. Negative no. 100506. Photo: Ferenz Fedor.

Fig. 41. *La Carretta de la Muerte,* 1986, by Luis Tapia, carved aspen with mica, human hair and teeth, and pony tail holder. Collection: The National Museum of American Art, Smithsonian Institution.

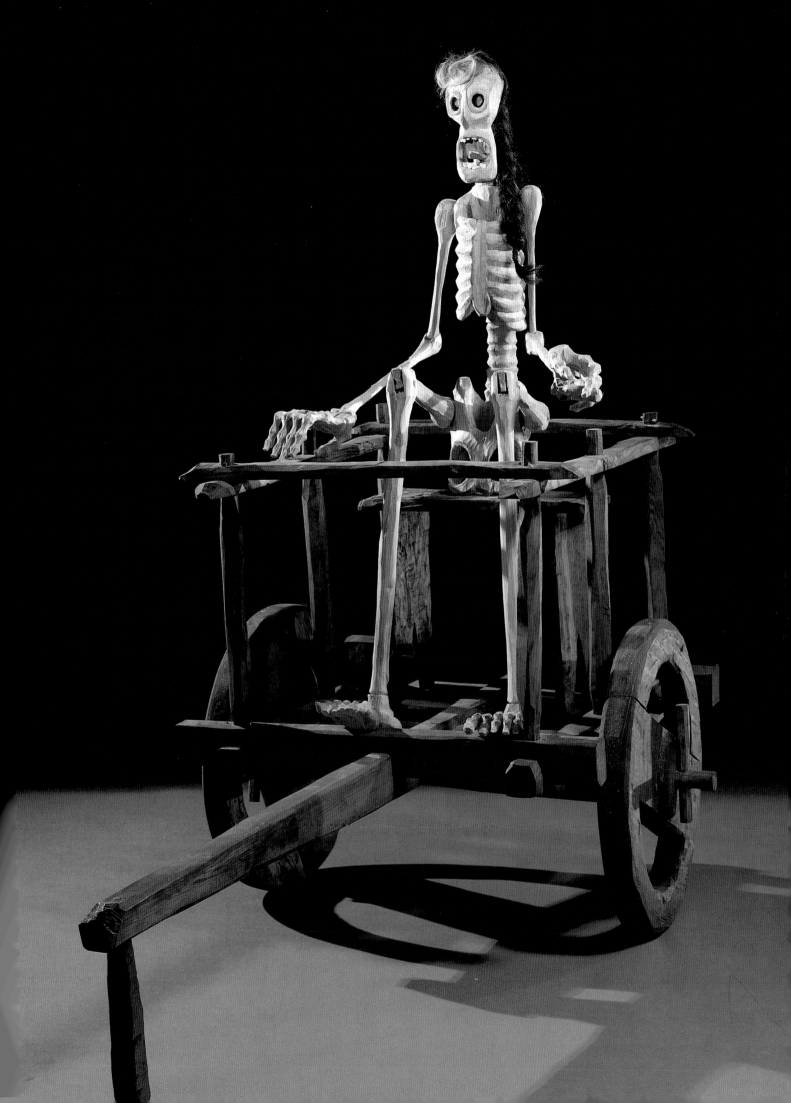

Fig. 42. San Ysidro church interior, with *reredos* donated by Luis Tapia, 1992, Agua Fría. Courtesy Franklin D. Pretto. Photo: Mary Peck.

Although Tapia may agree to create or restore altar screens in a Spanish colonial style, he does not entirely abide by the principles that guide many Anglo preservationist restoration efforts. With its modernist implications of redeeming something that is lost and representing it as one's own, preservation is a form of hegemonic appropriation that is irrelevant to Tapia's relationship to his culture.[30] Even when Tapia produces works of "art" for museum exhibitions, as he did for the Houston Fine Arts Center show, he maintains ties to his religion and his local community. In a carreta (wooden cart with a figure of death) he carved for the exhibition, Tapia used his children's teeth and Wilberto Miera's *chongo* (long braid) to dress the skeletal figure of Doña Sebastiana. Doña Sebastiana is the death figure who rides in the cart pulled in processions toward a designated Calvary during Holy Week by members of the Brotherhood of Our Father Jesus. Although museums ordinarily identify the materials used in works of art in their exhibition label copy, Tapia felt he could not divulge the names of either his children or Miera in any description of the carreta. He may not have made the Death Cart for religious purposes, but it still represented a sacred expression. In the Catholic religion, it is sacrilege to associate humans with religious images. Tapia may have welcomed the opportunity to create his own interpretation of a historic form, but when it came to the possibility of defacing his religion by naming human associations, he argued good-naturedly, "I'm not that contemporary."

Tapia also held a reverent attitude toward a reredos he made for the "Hispanic Art in the United States" exhibition. Whereas he left the altar screens he made for the San Ildefonso and Ranchos de Taos churches unsigned, he signed the one he made for the Houston show. On the lower frame bordering the bottom center panel of this screen, he wrote, *Este Altar Hiso Luis Tapia Año de 1986* (This altar was made by Luis Tapia in the year 1986). The way Tapia signed the screen—a simple sentence providing identification of the piece, the name of the maker, and the date of completion—recalls the phrasing on some Spanish colonial screens and retablos, where the name of the patron who subsidized the painting or the artist who donated his work was inscribed on one of the cartouches.[31] Although this form of signature was considered a sign of vanity, some carvers occasionally practiced it.

Tapia produced pieces for the Houston show at the request of the exhibition curators, but he did not receive commissions. He agreed to make the carvings on the condition that he could do with them as he pleased once the exhibition tour finished. Tapia intended to take the screen back to New Mexico and donate it to a church. He made the carreta available for sale. Eventually, the National Museum of American Art purchased the carreta. Today, Tapia's altar screen is installed in the San Isidro Church, in Agua Fría, where the artist grew up. According to Tapia, the members of the church "seem real happy with it." After he placed the altar screen in the church, Tapia dedicated it to the memory of his father.

Professional preservationists have designated the San Isidro Church as historically significant. Built in 1836, the structure is made in the Spanish colonial technique of stacked adobe bricks and mud plastered walls with a ceiling of *latillas* (small peeled poles used as lath), vigas, and corbels. The local community still worships in the church. An official scenic historic marker stands along the highway next to the church, for visitors and other passersby.

The artworks that Tapia produced for the Houston show now have places

Fig. 43. *La Cruz de Animas* (The Cross of the Souls), 1993, by Luis Tapia. Private collection. Courtesy Owings-Dewey Fine Art. Photo: Dan Morse.

CRAFTING DEVOTIONS

Fig. 44. *Los Hermanos at Sangre de Cristo*
(The Brothers at the Sangre de Cristo
Mountains), 1987, by Paul Pletka, oil on
canvas. Courtesy Museum of Fine Arts,
Museum of New Mexico, promised gift of
Dr. Luther W. Brady. Photo: Blair Clark.

of permanence, one in an ecclesiastical setting and the other in an environmentally controlled storage area of a museum. Ironically, the church's altar screen, on permanent public display in a building visited for its "traditional" construction, has more sightseers than the carreta stored in the National Museum of American Art. Visitors come to San Isidro Church not only to pray but also to see a representation of a traditional religious context. In Washington, D.C., the carreta sits in storage, devoid of "cultural" associations, imprisoned in darkness, and cherished as a masterpiece of Western art. Held sacred by professional culture managers, the carreta, with the exception of brief appearances in museum galleries, is protected from the public by the necessities of dimmed lighting and preventive maintenance. In the museum the carreta becomes a private, devotional object. In the church the altar screen enjoys the status of a hallowed museum masterpiece.

ALIGNMENTS

Although Luis Tapia grounds his santos and other wood carvings in northern New Mexico Hispano folklife, his association with the craft has evolved into an opportunity to make and remake himself within a living, changing tradition. Although, as Chicano studies scholar Tomás Ybarra-Frausto suggests, the fine-art world continues to uphold stereotypical notions of Hispano folk art as primitivistic and "folkloristic," Tapia views the thread of continuity in the wood-carving trade as a source of vitality and continuing maturation.[32] He uses the knowledge he has collected in ways that allow him to produce his own innovative carvings and paintings. For him, tradition is not static.

Tapia believes that the path to perpetuating tradition requires being true to himself. Cultural integrity implies personal integrity. Ethnographic method and vernacular religion and crafts provide a means for revising identity and culture. More than a documenter of folk culture, Tapia considers himself one of its creators.

Tapia has aligned his feelings about cultural and personal integrity with the work of Paul Pletka, a contemporary Anglo painter trained in a Western fine-art tradition who lives and works in New Mexico. A relatively young artist, Pletka paints in the tradition of inspired realism. A meticulous researcher, Pletka both depicts Western Hispano and Native American objects accurately and reinterprets them. Primarily taken with items of ritual, religion, and spiritual transformation, Pletka explores these tangible forms in an effort to reveal a new interpretation of history.[33]

When I asked Tapia how he felt about Pletka's selection of Hispano and Native American images for his painting, he replied, "I don't see why you can't [paint them. Pletka] doesn't try to pawn [his art] off as Hispano or Indian work. [Rather,] he can relate to it what he sees and understands in life." According to Tapia, "It doesn't bother me—using [Hispano and Native American] imagery; it's when you misrepresent yourself." Charles Carrillo has also aligned himself with Pletka.[34] According to Carrillo, Pletka has "been very careful about his research . . . [and is] doing a good job of telling us who we are."

Pletka's artistic method—the serious study of the history of the West embellished with personal interpretation—parallels that of Tapia and Carrillo. Tapia has conducted field work with northern villagers; Carrillo has done library and museum collection research on colonial santo construction. Like Pletka, both wood-carvers are urban middle-class artists who use the knowledge they have acquired to reinvent the traditions they have claimed. When Carrillo says that Pletka does "a good job of telling us who we are," he speaks less to a pedantic, imposing, or dominant quality of the artist than to an expressive technique that offers a broad framework in which to examine tradition.[35]

Luis Tapia takes his concern with integrity and self-representation very much to heart. Although he accepts being called a santero, he also qualifies his identification with the term. "I've learned to use the word for myself, but I work in a variety of media," Tapia told an NPR reviewer.[36] Recently, when I asked Tapia what he preferred to be called, he answered, "I'm a santero, but that's not all that I am. I'm a furniture maker, but that's not all that I am. What am I? I'm a sculptor."

When I asked Tapia why some carvers refer to saints as santos and others call them statues, he explained that "saints have a religious dimension, but they're not necessarily religious." Accordingly, the term *santo*, viewed by at least two scholars as an "arty byword," could be the word reserved for those saints that are "not necessarily religious."[37] Tapia refers to the saints he produces as santos, and although he practices Catholicism and considers himself a religious man, what he calls "the art part" of saint making compels him to carve.

Charles Carrillo also uses the word santero in his own way. He began painting retablos and carving bultos in the early 1980s, based on his interest in the folklore and religion of his colonial ancestors. Carrillo's family descends from Spanish colonists who settled the area in the sixteenth century and includes *genizaros* (detribalized Indians) on all four sides. He grew up in the urban center of Albuquerque and has only a limited speaking knowledge of Spanish. Despite his narrow exposure to rural Hispano life as a child, Carrillo immersed himself in the folk traditions of Hispano New Mexican Catholicism before he began carving santos. In 1977, while in the village of Abiquiu doing field work toward a Ph.D. in archaeology, Carrillo became a member of the Abiquiu Brotherhood of Our Father Jesus. He also met his wife there. In the summer of 1990, Carrillo won the grand prize at the Santa Fe Spanish Market. His image of San Ysidro, the patron saint of farmers and a much celebrated santo among rural Hispano New Mexicans, won.

Like Tapia, Carrillo is involved in conflicts between and among tradition bearers and culture managers, in this case members of various brotherhood tribunals and contemporary santeros, Spanish colonial folk-art scholars, and other interested museum personnel. Carrillo believes in a strong connection between his membership in the Abiquiu cofradía and his work as a santero. He views both as "keepers of tradition." On the other hand, Carrillo's brothers in the Abiquiu morada (brotherhood meetinghouse) disagree. They occasionally reprimand him for producing ritual objects for an outside market. In response, Carrillo argues, as the Córdovan carver George López did before him, that none of the santos are sacred objects until they are blessed.[38] Carrillo regrets that politics and an unquestioning adherence to the privacy of Penitente rituals prevent some members of the brotherhood from an objective appreciation of the beauty of their material expressions, but he also values his association with the brotherhood. According to Carrillo, "Without their spiritual inspiration, I wouldn't be who I am." Carrillo's "biggest influence has been the brotherhood."

Carrillo emphasizes the relevance of the brotherhood to contemporary life by mentioning that more and more *hermanos* (members of the brother-

Fig. 45. *San Ysidro Labradór*, 1990, by Charles
M. Carrillo. Grand prize winner, 1990 Spanish
Market, Ponderosa pine, cottonwood root,
rawhide, horsehair, gourd, natural pigments.
Collection: Gene Autry Western Heritage
Museum. Photo: Susan Einstein.

< **Fig. 46.** Living room of Carrillo home, Santa Fe, summer 1992. In the weeks before Spanish Market, patrons come to Carrillo's home for a preview of what the artist plans to bring to the market. Carrillo artfully and reverentially displays his new santos amidst older santos in his personal collection. For example, on a reclining nineteenth-century Guatemalan image of the Niño (Christ child), Carrillo strews decorative *ramilletes* (paper cut-outs) made by his daughter Estrellita. On a shelf above the wooden bench, Carrillo arranges old and new santos with accoutrements seen on religious altars, such as doilies. Along with creating these devotional displays, Carrillo stores business cards for himself and other family members, anticipating greeting patrons at Spanish Market. Before Spanish Market, Carrillo's living room becomes an exhibition of the many worlds the artist inhabits. Photo: Mary Peck.

Fig. 47. Luis Tapia and three of his abstract carvings in stone and wood, Santa Fe, 1988. Photo: Mary Peck.

hood) are now santeros. Some brothers, such as Nicolás Herrera of El Rito, have become well known as artists, thanks to their participation in the Spanish Market. Carrillo views the contemporary hermanos' loyalty to Penitente rituals as a preservationist enterprise. He also believes it is only natural for them to become santeros. This is the only way, he claims, that they can reinvolve themselves with their culture. Reflecting on his membership in these varied worlds, Carrillo asks of himself, "Can I be honest to my own people, to my tradition? Can I feed my children? I don't like to make price tags the most important part of [my santos]." As he struggles to integrate the diverse elements of his experience into a unified whole, Carrillo argues that, historically, *hermanos* and santeros were the same. At the very least, they shared a harmonious relationship.

Like Carrillo and Pletka, Luis Tapia struggles with a variety of aesthetic and cultural conventions to find his own place in the world. For the past twelve years, he has enjoyed carving modernist-style abstract and figurative sculpture along with his santos, altar screens, and furniture. He has experimented with stone as well as with local woods such as juniper, Russian olive, and walnut to produce carvings that have little connection to Spanish colonial folk art. Instead, the carvings, many of which are life-size, depict elongated female nudes or birds, or they are abstract works not easily identified. Unlike the frontal, static, and geometric santos he carves, these sculptures, all of which Tapia calls "abstract," suggest motion and evoke a sense of liberation and freedom.

When Tapia begins to carve one of his abstracts, he professes that he doesn't "even know what [he's] going to do." Although he claims that the images for these works are in his head, he also says that the "wood is pulling that image

out of [him] rather than [him] pulling it out of the wood."[39] With a picture in his mind of what he'd like to carve, Tapia lets the size of the wood and its grain determine the piece's end result. Other contemporary santeros who produce abstracts along with santos share this attitude, which resembles that of such modernist primitivists as Constantin Brancusi and Henry Moore. Brancusi and Moore followed the tenet of "truth to materials," which had an almost ethical tone. According to art critic Robert Goldwater, this notion suggests a "sense of respect for the medium, a feeling that its inherent qualities of grain or crystalline structure, its limits of stress and strain, must not be violated."[40] The sculptors found these qualities in what they called "primitive" art, in wood and stone carvings from Africa, Oceania, and Mexico.

Whereas, however, Brancusi and, to a lesser extent, Moore deliberately and romantically maintained rough and unrefined surfaces in some of their sculpture, Tapia consciously and constantly works hard at smoothing the exterior of his work. In his wood carvings, Brancusi put a calculated emphasis on what he believed was simply an unavoidable condition of aboriginal sculpture's physical existence, but Tapia intentionally labors to produce refined, modern fine-art sculpture.[41]

Tapia creates his abstracts with less of a profit motive than he does his religious art or furniture. When he discusses his abstract carvings, he talks about leaving behind the pieces he makes for hire and instead getting back to doing his "own work." To Tapia, his own work includes abstract sculpture. Often, he does his abstracts on a large scale; they therefore differ in size as well as in subject matter and form from santos. The santos typically range from fifteen to eighteen

Fig. 48. Owings-Dewey Fine Art display of Luis Tapia's work, 1991. Photo: Miguel A. Gandert.

CRAFTING DEVOTIONS

inches in height. Tapia is not opposed to the idea of selling his abstracts. In fact, some of them have been available through Owings-Dewey Fine Art. Rather, he maintains that the conditions he sets for making his abstract sculpture, his deference to the integrity of the wood's grain, are not necessarily compatible with the specific needs of patrons.

Tapia's verbal agreement to sell his work exclusively through Owings-Dewey Fine Art has proven successful for the artist and the gallery. A restrictive artist and gallery association, in which the dealer sells whatever the artist produces, negates the need for the artist to work on commission. The artist creates what he chooses and delivers his finished product to the gallery, which then tries to sell it. For Tapia, this relationship provides more opportunity to do his own work, to experiment with innovative decorative techniques on furniture and explore new subject matter for santos, as well as to carve abstract sculpture. Also, a gallery association means that Tapia no longer must deal with the financial or publicity aspects of his work. To know that the gallery staff will care for his clients allows Tapia to concentrate solely on his carving. Consequently, he reaps steady and substantial financial rewards from this association. Even with a significant markup in price, the gallery sells all of Tapia's work. The dealer and the artist both make a large profit.

Although Tapia began his carving career out of political motivation and an awakened sense of his own ethnicity, much of the current discussion surrounding his work focuses on aesthetics. According to Nat Owings, who owns Owings-Dewey Fine Art, the gallery handles Tapia's work because Tapia is the only contemporary santero whose carving "approximates fine art." As little for-

< **Fig. 49.** Interior, Luis Tapia's studio, Santa Fe, 1988. Photo: Mary Peck.

Fig. 50. *Noah's Ark,* 1991, by Luis Tapia. Collection: Joan Richman. Courtesy Owings-Dewey Fine Art.

◄ **Fig. 51.** *Tribute to Maria Benítez,* 1990, by Luis Tapia. A native Taoseño, María Benítez is considered by many to be the world's finest flamenco dancer. Collection: Gene Autry Western Heritage Museum. Photo: Susan Einstein.

Fig. 52. *"Spanish Colonial" Carretta,* 1993, by Luis Tapia, 10 1/4" x 14" x 3". Collection: Terry and Eva Herndon. Courtesy Owings-Dewey Fine Art. Photo: Dan Morse.

mal connection exists, however, between the early-twentieth-century landscape and still-life paintings of the Taos and Santa Fe artists also handled by Owings-Dewey Fine Art and Tapia's brightly painted religious images, Owings's reasoning seems invented. By handling Tapia's work in his gallery, Owings undeniably promotes the santero's work from something of cultural value to something of artistic value, but the owner's decision to take on the sale of this work ultimately has little to do with aesthetics. Rather, one might argue, it has more to do with economics. Tapia's prior participation in "Hispanic Art in the United States: Thirty Contemporary Painters and Sculptors" and his subsequent popularity in the mainstream art world offer the promise of orders for carvings and furniture by elite art collectors. These are the very patrons who already frequent Owings's gallery.

Although the arrangement with Owings-Dewey Fine Art appears to allow Tapia considerable expressive freedom, the market and the gallery owner ultimately control his production. Tapia may prefer the term *sculptor* over others, but the carvings he considers sculpture are the ones least available for sale in the gallery. Although Tapia says he is eager to work more on his abstracts, Nat Owings claims that Tapia is getting away from carving his large, unpainted figurative and nonrepresentational pieces. Whether Owings's statement about Tapia's abstracts is accurate, such works rarely appear in the gallery. At Owings-Dewey Fine Art, patrons consider santos and furniture as art. They have no category for Tapia's abstract carvings.

Associating Tapia with the terms *sculptor* and *sculpture* is meaningless at Owings-Dewey Fine Art. It is equally out of place away from the gallery. As Tapia talks, in a sawdust-covered workshop filled with Spanish colonial furniture in various states of disrepair, about his abstracts and his nude sculpture, I am reminded of the stately wording of inscriptions found on the religious panels of the early-nineteenth-century santero José Aragón. Although Aragón's painted santos resembled the geometric, two-dimensional "folk" style of other colonial santeros, his use of words such as *pintureria* (painting), *esculteria* (sculpture studio) and *muestrario* (exhibition or demonstration of) in his signatures reflected a more formal vocabulary than other New Mexicans used at the time.[42] It reflected exposure to the Western art world without true access to its tenets.

In 1989, Tapia began carving nondenominational santos, expanding his repertoire for the gallery. Referring to an image he made of Noah's Ark, Tapia explains that he wants to get away from carving only Catholic saints. He claims that many of the visitors who come to Owings-Dewey Fine Art are Jews from the East Coast. They like Tapia's work, but they have no affinity for Catholic art. According to anthropologists John Bodine and Sylvia Rodríguez, the particular brand of Hispano folk Catholicism practiced in northern New Mexico engenders more prejudice and fear among outsiders than admiration.[43] Tomás Ybarra-Frausto claims that Catholicism is one of the constituent elements of Hispano art selectively ignored by collectors and dealers.[44] Ethnicity is more popular than religion among buyers of Hispano art. Consequently, Tapia has begun another secular form of image making—carvings of popular Hispano musicians and dancers, such as Flaco Jiménez and Maria Benítez.

Just as Tapia's business arrangement with Owings-Dewey Fine Art affects the types of carvings he makes, so have his various work spaces also influenced his work. From the early to mid-1980s, Tapia shared a rental space in a commercial strip of buildings in Santa Fe with the well-known Anglo artist Gary

Mauro. Mauro, whose work is shown mostly in Taos, produces large cotton quilted images of nude women. When Tapia shared a work space with Mauro, he began to experiment with carving life-size female nudes. And just as Mauro worked with models for his designs, so did Tapia attempt to carve a figure from photographs he had taken of a dancer. Because of the primacy Tapia gives his wood, he would only use photographs of models as prototypes if they could accommodate the grain and the size of his wood. Thus, Tapia's adherence, albeit unschooled, to modernist ideals of relying on the organic nature of materials combines with his connection to members of the trendy, largely Anglo New Mexico art scene and lends credence to his statement, "Hispano or not, I am concerned with the [artistic] development of my work."

Luis Tapia's connections to local and national fine art communities, museums, and diverse regional Chicano artists are more extensive than those of other contemporary New Mexico santeros. Tapia has been invited twice to the Smithsonian Institution's Festival of American Folklife to demonstrate wood carving; and he has traveled to Houston, Los Angeles, and New York, following the tour of "Hispanic Art in the United States," demonstrating furniture making for a department store and attending openings of museum and gallery shows of works by Chicano artists. Especially through a friendship he developed with Los Angeles artist and activist Gilbert Luján (Magu), whom he met during their participation in "Hispanic Art in America," Tapia has discovered new political and aesthetic alliances that reach beyond the confines of the Rio Grande village communities and Santa Fe barrio. He has spent months at a time sharing studio space with Gilbert Luján in Hollywood, California.

Tapia believes that "things are getting easier" for him now. The urgency to remind the local art community that they have neglected Hispano art has subsided. Whereas patrons and other artists once visited Tapia in his workshop to discuss his artwork and share news of other carvers, the artist now prefers his privacy. He'd rather be working. He has an exclusive arrangement with one of the most reputable dealers in town, and his work is exhibited nationally. Finally, after more than fifteen years of working in wood, Tapia has gained artistic acceptance, on what he considers his own terms.

2

PRIMITIVISM, MODERNISM, AND PATROCINIO BARELA

Bulto of San Antonio (Saint Anthony), 1991, by José Benjamín López. Detail of fig. 67.

FINE ART CRITICS have compared the carvings Patrocinio Barela produced (primarily in the 1930s and 1940s) to the native arts of Africa and Oceania. Carved in cedar or white pine and left unpainted, the individual faces of Barela's carvings are bilaterally symmetrical, like most folk art, but generally, the sculptures resemble more closely the rhythmic complexity of much of tribal art.[1] The carvings are symbolic in formal representation, rendered in forceful outline with little attention to detail. Heads are the most articulated parts of the carvings. They share protruding foreheads, long, straight noses, and slits for eyes. The torsos, when they are carved, are fashioned in a frontal position.[2]

Collectors and connoisseurs not only confer a "primitive" status on Barela's carvings but also directly link the form of his work to the tribal statues that Picasso, Brancusi, Modigliani, Henry Moore, and other early-twentieth-century artists collected and referred to in their paintings and sculpture. And like the anonymous wood-carvers from Africa and the Pacific Islands who inspired the modernists, Barela had little knowledge of the praise Western critics bestowed on him.

In his day, Patrocinio Barela was controversial. His unconventional and nontraditional wood carvings made a significant impression on the elite modern-art world. But they alienated many members of his own community. The wood-carver's personal history tainted native perceptions of him. Born in 1908 in Bisbee, Arizona, the son of a somewhat wayward *curandero* (folk healer), Barela did not possess the long family lineage in which Hispanos in Taos, his eventual home, take pride.[3] An itinerant laborer for many years and a heavy

Opposite

Fig. 53. Wood carving, n.d., Patrocinio Barela. Collection: Dr. and Mrs. J. O. Domínguez. Photo: Mary Peck.

Fig. 54. Patrocinio Barela in his studio, n.d. Courtesy Trinnie and Luis Barela, Sr. Photographer unknown.

drinker, he was also unable to meet the financial and other responsibilities necessary to care for himself or his family. He did not incorporate into his own life the domestic ideology so prominent among Hispanos in Taos. As a result, members of the local community looked askance at Barela. Some even considered him a bit *loco* (crazy).[4]

But over the past twenty years, Hispano Taoseños and other native New Mexicans have reversed their attitudes toward Patrocinio Barela and his work. Now relatives and townspeople who knew the carver speak with reverence about him. And contemporary santeros who never met the man have turned the illiterate, alcoholic wood-carver into a contemporary Chicano hero. Where Barela once was ignored by his neighbors, today he is embraced by his fans. Critics, neighbors, and family members now celebrate his carvings as possibly the most important Hispano art produced in the twentieth century.[5]

More than a few contemporary santeros make what they call "abstract" or "modernistic" carvings, along with the santos, furniture, and painted animals they carve. Sometimes carvers link their abstracts directly to Barela. Patrocinio's own grandson, Luis Barela, Jr., recently moved back to Taos County from Texas to produce replicas of his grandfather's carvings.

Although contemporary carvers of abstract sculpture claim a personal aesthetic and political motivation for their work, they work in a shared repertory of abstract forms. These carvers may work individually, but some of them meet regularly to discuss their projects and ideas. Like Luis Tapia, they rely on local woods such as juniper, Russian olive, and walnut. And they use the same types of hand tools to produce a finite variety of figurative and nonfigurative forms.

The unpainted carvings range in size from about sixteen inches to larger than life. The heads are often geometric in design and have protruding foreheads and slits for eyes and mouths. Sometimes, like Barela's work, one figurative carving may have more than one head. Some have more than one body. As with Barela's carvings, critics and connoisseurs often compare contemporary Hispano abstracts to the art of Africa and Oceania. Today's Hispano abstractionists themselves frequently liken their work to early-twentieth-century modernist sculpture and to the carvings of Barela.

This chapter is about Barela, the early artists and neighbors who admired him, and the contemporary Hispanos who produce their own images based on Barela's work. I explore how Barela's wood carvings and historical attitudes about the carver have a heightened significance for New Mexicans, specifically santeros. To understand this, I compare Barela's works with contemporary santeros' abstract sculpture in an effort to examine how the carvers have used Barela as a model. I discuss individual santeros' motivations for making abstract art, and I also chart the development of the notion of abstract art among the carvers. Although many contemporary santeros use Barela's work as inspiration for their own innovative expression, I suggest that it is not only Barela the artist who has value for contemporary santeros. It is also the modernist aesthetic and praise that have attached themselves to the idea of Barela.

PATROCINIO BARELA

Little information exists about Patrocinio Barela's life. Most newspaper and magazine articles about the wood-carver appeared after his death. Three Anglo Taoseños published a book on Barela; however, they transcribed the carver's remarks using a poetic form that followed their own literary aesthetics.[6] Barela, himself illiterate, left no written records.

A partial reconstruction of Barela's life is possible, but at best it can only be told as an assemblage of stories. A newspaper article from the *Taos News* attests to this:

> Patrocinio Barela? The man's a genius. He has a head like Goya, and the talent of a Rodin.
>
> Patrocinio Barela? The man's a stinker. I threw him out of my shop once.
>
> Patrocinio Barela? Wonderful, wonderful. Invest some money in his better works. You'll sell them for a fortune one day.
>
> Ask any ten Taoseños about Pat Barela and you'll get ten different reactions.[7]

Those Anglo aesthetes of Taos who thought about Barela at all believed only they comprehended him. They report that Barela's wife, Remedios, was a constant source of frustration, and even antagonism, for her husband.[8] Some criticized Remedios and the Barela children for being unsympathetic to the wood-carver's craft, selling it when they needed cash for clothing and other necessities, or even for entertainment, such as going to the movies. [9]

Two of Barela's children, Julia and Luis, Sr., still live in the Taos area. A third child, Robert, died in 1976. Today, Julia and Luis, Sr., are happy to discuss their father; they portray him in a positive, indeed inspirational, light. The children's current celebration of their father, however, is at times so indistinguishable from today's widespread appreciation of Barela that it is difficult to determine their original feelings.

Fig. 55. Nude, n.d., by José Benjamín López. Collection of the artist. Photo: Mary Peck.

The difficulty in obtaining a consistent portrait of Patrocinio Barela may have something to do with his elusive personality, but it also has to do with the class structure and ethnic relations in Taos at the time the artist worked. Unlike other primarily Mexicano towns in northern New Mexico, Taos was, and remains, a cultural crossroads. In the early twentieth century, Anglo artists and patrons moved to Taos from the East Coast and Europe and essentially colonized the region according to their own aesthetic, intellectual, and political interests. Although these "ethnicity seekers" came to Taos because of what they saw as its exotic foreign population, the Anglo artists and patrons nevertheless disturbed the tenor of relationships between the Indians and Spanish who lived there before them.[10] Whereas they favored the Taos Indians for what they considered their "immutably mysterious culture," the Anglo immigrants regarded Hispanos or Mexicans as "an afflicted, somehow blameworthy source of social irritation or danger, a kind of folk who were really a class."[11] As a result of the Anglo prejudice against them and the concurrent glorification of the Indians, Hispanos developed resentment toward both the Indians and the Anglos. Nevertheless, economic pressures and the tourism industry required the Taos Hispano community to accommodate themselves to the demands and needs of both these ethnic groups.

During the 1940s and 1950s, Anglo doctors, war veterans, local businessmen, and other professionals launched a campaign to "civilize" Taos, to bring it technologically into the mid-twentieth century. The Taos Hispano community came under increasing pressure to suppress its culture, to give up local, nonindustrial, and otherwise traditional ways in favor of technological progress and Anglo behavior patterns.[12] Against this backdrop, Patrocinio Barela carved. He persisted in doing something that the community was then being forced to ignore. Because Barela's carvings were more abstract than the realist santos so familiar to the local population, both his native group and Anglo immigrants saw him as a threat. Patrocinio Barela defied the social structure of mid-twentieth-century Taos. But he was not a born leader, and he had no command of the English language. Instead of a hero, he became a victim of his time.

All reports tell us that Barela started carving by making saints. According to Luis Barela, Jr., "They say [Patrocinio] started by fixing a santo put together with joints, and that inspired him to find a way to do it all out of one piece. What he liked carving was things just in the wood, whatever he saw."[13] Another version says that in 1931, the carver was attracted to an old santo in need of repair. The night he saw the bulto, he became so excited by it that he went home and immediately began to carve a head from a stick of wood.[14]

Although he quickly switched to carving unpainted figurative and abstract juniper sculpture, some writers claim that Barela needed convincing that his unconventional carvings had enough worth for him to stop making his religious images.[15] The convincing Barela received, however, only had meaning for members of the Anglo art world who offered it. It had little meaning for Barela's wife. According to one WPA writer, Remedios gathered up six early santos of Patrocinio's and "traded the lot for some used clothing which was of very little value."[16] The writer neglected to mention, however, that used clothing could have had far more appeal and value to a woman with both a family to feed and dress and constant pressure from the very culture trying to preserve her husband's "art" to assimilate into modern life.

Fig. 56. Wood carving, n.d., Patrocinio Barela. Collection: Dr. and Mrs. J. O. Domínguez. Photo: Mary Peck.

CRAFTING DEVOTIONS

Barela and the Taos Art Colony

By the 1930s, when Barela first began to carve, newcomers to New Mexico had taken possession of the term *native* and all the cultural idioms that went with it. For Eastern aesthetes who journeyed West, Santa Fe and Taos became America's Orient—a place of romance, exotic beings, haunting memories and landscapes, remarkable experiences.[17] In search of spiritual inspiration, Anglo artists and writers looked to New Mexico as a source of "fresh material" for their work.[18] Moreover, because of a fusion of American capitalism and creativity at the turn of the century, Anglo fascination with exotic New Mexico became a type of corporate institution wherein the Anglo-American power elite produced authoritative views about the Southwest.[19]

Anglo fascination with the "otherness" of New Mexico manifested itself in three major ways. First, American- and European-trained artists learned from friends of what they described as the moral and spiritual virtues of New Mexico and either visited or settled there permanently. Steeped in fine-art traditions of realism and modernism, early-twentieth-century artists considered Hispano and Indian cultures as useful subject matter for expressing their values and ideals.[20]

Second, the New Mexico tourist industry, the State Highway Department, the Atchison, Topeka and Santa Fe Railway, and others discovered the economic potential of the Indians, Hispanos, and Anglo artists as tourist attractions. They capitalized on local celebrations such as fiestas, as well as fine-art paintings of native life, and mounted elaborate advertising campaigns that lured people to the Southwest.[21]

Third, Anglo writers, artists, educators, and patrons established classes in vocational schools and set up markets to perpetuate the production and sale of native crafts. For example, in the 1920s, Mary Austin and Frank Applegate founded the Spanish Colonial Arts Society, to "encourage and promote" and "preserve and revive" Spanish colonial art. In 1934, Leonora Curtin opened the Native Market in Santa Fe, intended as a sales outlet for the many students studying Spanish colonial craftsmanship in outlying vocational schools.[22] By the 1920s and 1930s, art, business, and tourism in New Mexico established a substantive and mutually supportive relationship.[23] Although these native-art enthusiasts' and promoters' intentions may have emanated from a spiritual, democratic, or aesthetic impulse to counter racial or ethnic prejudice and improve the economic situation of native groups, their efforts were ultimately self-serving.[24]

Although Barela may have been pigeonholed as a native artist, his abstract carvings, resembling modern sculpture more than traditional santos, had no place within the local artistic milieu. Grounded in Catholicism, yet more abstract in their rendering and more universal in their subject matter, Barela's wood carvings were perceived by the mainstream art world to extend beyond religious dogma in content and form.[25] By 1939, Barela's carvings were displayed at the New York World's Fair, included in Federal Art Project Director Holger Cahill's exhibition "New Horizons in American Art," and purchased for the permanent collection of the Museum of Modern Art. Still, Barela continued to be ignored, exploited, or, at best, misunderstood at home. Early-twentieth-century artists who came to New Mexico had little use for African-style sculpture done by a person they considered a native. Rather, they sought out santos, Indian pottery, and the accoutrements of rural, agrarian life.

Although Barela was virtually neglected by the mainstream Anglo art world in Taos, certain cosmopolitan gallery owners, such as Eulalia Emetaz, attempted to work with the carver. Because of the carvings' formal resemblance to tribal sculpture, Emetaz elevated them over other local, native examples of material culture and attempted to sell them as art. Ultimately, however, the business relationship between Barela and Emetaz failed. Emetaz allowed the carver to depend on her for money,[26] but she required a type of negotiation that Barela could not honor. She asked that Barela not change the prices she attached to the bottom of his carvings rather than sell the pieces for less money when he needed it or barter them for wine. When Barela could not keep to this arrangement, he and Emetaz parted ways.[27]

With little recognition of the "ethnic trap" in which Barela found himself—where he was required to conduct business within dominant culture guidelines that had little meaning for him—members of the Taos Anglo art world described the carver's alcoholism as a barrier to effective communication. One Taos gallery employee claims that Barela was impossible to work with. She remembers him as a "nice man," but certainly not as a recognized, upstanding member of any community in Taos. Typically, he could be found in town on the plaza, she says, drinking wine with the Taos Indians. According to the employee, Barela was not someone with whom members of the Taos art colony kept company.

Thomas Merlan, raised in Taos and currently director of the State Historic Preservation Division in Santa Fe, explains that "the 1930s, 1940s, and 1950s Taos artists were social elite. They weren't interested in a local illiterate artist who hauled wood. . . . It didn't occur to the Taos art community that [Barela] was an artist." Barela did not paint landscapes, favored by many of the New Mexico modernists, nor did he socialize in the homes of artists or patrons in the evenings. He had no opportunity to cross paths with the elite artists who came to Taos to escape a larger cosmopolitan world. Members of the Taos Anglo art world considered Barela one of the locals. They dismissed his behavior as lower-class.

NEIGHBORS

Although many Anglo Taos art colonists ignored Barela, certain local community members developed a strong appreciation for the artist. Dr. J. A. Domínguez, a Taos osteopath, speaks familiarly and affectionately about Barela. Their relationship was originally based on proximity rather than on aesthetics. Domínguez and Barela lived near each other in Cañon, and Remedios Barela worked as a domestic for the Domínguez family. Domínguez purchased carvings from Barela more in an effort to be neighborly than to participate in the sort of salvaging so valued by the fine-art world.

Domínguez does not romanticize Barela's temperament. He remembers that Barela slapped and kicked his wife, and he acknowledges the woodcarver's alcoholism. Still, Domínguez recognizes a visionary quality about the carver. He claims, "People say Pat smoked pot. . . . [I don't] think artists and anybody else took [Barela] seriously. . . . He was so ugly and so unshaven, but," Domínguez continues, "[he] had the talent, you couldn't help but admire him. . . . To look at [him], you'd think he was thinking all the time."

Unlike other collectors of Southwest native art, Domínguez has no personal collection spanning a wide range of historic and ethnographic artifacts. He simply owns lots of Barelas. By purchasing a group of Barela sculptures for his personal edification, Domínguez joined in the act of turning local wood carving into valuable art. By disregarding, on the other hand, the prestige associated

OVERLEAF

Fig. 57. The Domínguezes' kitchen, Cañon, 1992. All the wood carvings displayed here are by Patrocinio Barela, with the exception of eight sculptures on the top shelf by John Suazo, a Taos Pueblo artist. Courtesy Dr. and Mrs. J. O. Domínguez. Photo: Mary Peck.

with amassing such a personal collection and its related social, commercial, and aesthetic opportunities, Domínguez maintains an oblique relationship to the elite art-culture system.

Like Domínguez, Barela also remained indifferent to the fine-art world. Yet he participated in it when it worked to his advantage. In at least one instance, Barela obliged a prodigious collector who wanted a piece of "primitive" New Mexican art by producing for him what fine-art connoisseurs might consider a fake.

According to Taoseño John Manchester, Barela was approached by an aristocratic Englishman named Edward James, who visited his cousin, the artist Lady Dorothy Brett, at her home in Taos between 1929 and 1930. Reportedly, James was the illegitimate son of King Edward VIII and quite wealthy in his own right. He collected a good deal of art, including the work of Salvador Dali, who had been his close friend. James was fascinated with "primitive" as well as "fine" art, and, on his first visit to Taos, he expressed an interest in acquiring an old Death Cart figure from a morada used by members of the Brotherhood of Our Father Jesus. Lady Brett and James approached Barela with their request, and the wood-carver promised to look for what Manchester described as "the requested piece of sculpture."

Some months later, Barela brought a Death Cart figure to Lady Brett and James. James was quite free with his money and probably paid Barela "a fair amount" for the work. Later, however, Lady Brett and James discovered that the Death Cart was not old, that in fact Barela had made the carving himself. Supposedly, he had buried it in manure for a couple of months to "antique" it.[28] On learning of Barela's fraud, James rejected the Death Cart as a fake.

When he left Taos, James gave the carving—no longer the "authentic masterpiece" he had at first thought it to be—to Lady Brett, who stored it in a pump house she shared with Manchester. Eventually, Lady Brett gave the carving to Manchester, who donated it to the Harwood Foundation in Taos in 1977. To Manchester, the Death Cart "always seemed a *rare* piece, . . . both because it was so early in Barela's carving career and for its large size."[29] Rather than an art forgery, as James saw it, Manchester considered the Barela Death Cart a "masterpiece." Authenticated by Lady Brett as a "real Barela," the Death Cart, first authentic, then a fake, then a genuine Barela, became worthy of a museum collection.

Jesse Merlan (1913–88), another neighbor who purchased Barela's works, considered the sculpture in terms of Western aesthetics. Although Merlan had little formal training in art history, his life experience was closer to the Taos art colonists than it was to local Hispano Taoseños like Dr. Domínguez. Jesse Merlan was educated at Columbia University and moved to Taos from New York. He was a successful cartoonist for the Superman comics series, was familiar with the tenets of modernism, and was Anglo. According to his son, Thomas, Jesse Merlan considered Barela's wood carving less as work by a talented local friend and more in terms of modern art. Merlan believed Barela initially grounded his carvings in the local santo tradition, but that they went through a radical simplification of form, approaching abstraction. To Merlan, Barela's wood carvings were "within boundaries . . . fixed by religion," but they were also universal and "highly, startlingly original."

Jesse Merlan saw his relationship to Barela as one of patron to artist. He invited the carver to work at his home and offered encouragement by showing him works by Gauguin and Van Gogh. Speaking about his father's attitude, Thomas Merlan says, "[Barela] was an artist. That's all he was. There was nothing else of significance."

Like Domínguez, Jesse Merlan had no romantic preconceptions about Barela. For example, he thought the wood-carver was a bad father. But Merlan also blamed Barela's precariousness on the fact that he was a victim—of poverty, racial inequities, drink, illness, and a family for whom carving had no place.

Much of the current talk about Barela centers on the way local Taoseños claim to have cared for him. They describe Barela as having been downtrodden, misunderstood, and vulnerable to exploitation. They contrast him with the self-described strong, upstanding, professional, mostly Anglo members of the community who had the "taste" to recognize the aesthetic value of his work.

In the late 1950s and early 1960s, the years just before he died, Barela was very ill from tubercular or tertiary syphilis. Thomas Merlan recalls his father buying medicine for Barela. Throughout his illness, Barela created pornographic sculpture, producing graphic representations of sexuality. Whether or not a connection exists between Barela's disease and those carvings, Thomas Merlan suggests an association between the carver's explicit anatomical works and his desire for his own type of medicine. Merlan claims that Barela sold the pornographic sculpture "when he needed a drink. They were a sure sell." Another neighbor of Barela's, Ben Tafoya, expresses a similar opinion, maintaining that Barela "worked for a living. When you look at pornographic stuff, it was probably a commission." According to Merlan and Tafoya, Barela's pornographic carvings were a means to economic survival. Following Sally Price's notion that Western culture links erotic symbolism with the life of "primitives,"[30] it is possible that Barela produced erotic sculpture in his Anglo patrons' images of local native art.

Whereas Merlan purchased medicine for Barela, other local patrons have been criticized for supporting the carver's alcoholism. Some people claim that a couple who owned a popular Taos inn in the 1940s and 1950s bought sculptures from Barela in exchange for cheap bottles of wine. Although the couple declares that they befriended the wood-carver, giving him beans and taking him home when he needed help getting there, others say "they just helped him to be a drunk."

Yet while this couple is criticized for exploiting a man now celebrated for being a great artist, the wife, who speaks fondly of Barela, remembers that the artist himself was ashamed of his carvings, calling them *monos* (literally, monkeys, but also, whimsical things).[31] And in spite of Barela's perhaps ambivalent attitude toward his work, this same woman also says that she actually helped Barela advance his career. She recalls how she taught Barela to write his name. Barela's signature, which either took the form of just the first three letters of his first name and surname, or the first three letters of his first name and his complete surname, subsequently appeared on the bottom of many of his carvings. According to the family member, this particular form of the signature distinguishes Barela's sculpture from replicas, many of which, she purports, exist. She claims, "If [the carvings are] signed in full, they're fake." Thomas Merlan also claims that "there are a lot of Barela fakes floating around." The ability to distinguish Barela carvings from replicas, connoisseurship, is another criterion Taoseños rely on to demonstrate their intimate familiarity with the wood-carver.

His local caretakers assumed that because of his lack of education, his alcoholism, and possibly his ethnicity, Barela had no appreciation of the artistry

Fig. 58. Doors made by Patrocinio Barela for artist Richard Dicus, Cañon, ca. 1941. Richard Dicus, Barela's neighbor, was an Anglo artist originally from Baltimore. He purchased a Spanish colonial hacienda in Cañon, building Spanish colonial–style additions onto it. Like Jesse Merlan, Dicus hired Barela to make wood carvings for him. These doors have five panels on each side, with relief carvings depicting everyday scenes in Taos. The lower right panel in this picture reads, "Carved by Pat Barela December 20, [1941?]." Courtesy William and Eudora Waugh. Photo: Mary Peck.

Fig. 59. Panel (detail) from door made by
Patrocinio Barela for Richard Dicus, Cañon, ca.
1941. The multistoried adobe structures with
ladders and dome-shaped *hornos* (ovens) on the
right, Catholic mission on the left, and
mountains in the background suggest that this is
a relief carving of Taos Pueblo. Courtesy William
and Eudora Waugh. Photo: Mary Peck.

Fig. 60. Wood carving, ca. 1930–40, by
Patrocinio Barela. The signature here, which
takes the form of the first three letters of the
first and last names, is considered one of the
carver's trademarks. Excepting a configuration
in which the first three letters of the first
name and the complete surname are spelled
out, connoisseurs and other aficionados
consider all other signatures as fake.
Collection: Gene Autry Western Heritage
Museum. Photo: Susan Einstein.

of his work. As a result, they took on the responsibility of recognizing it for him. In so doing, however, they stripped the man of his own origins or context. Today, Barela's neighbors remember him for praising the paintings of Van Gogh and damning his own work. Because of their own ideas, these neighbors bought Barela's works, and gave him food, money, and medicine. The couple criticized for exploiting the man even gave him his signature. At the same time that Barela's signature afforded his work entrance into the Western art world, it also deprived the carver of the "primitive," exotic, or mysterious quality, that is, the anonymous "otherness" for which the fine-art world originally recognized him. Further, the aesthetic values that critics and patrons attached to Barela's work clouded the untrained sculptor's own motivations for carving and the work's native meaning.

The hegemonic quality of their praise for Barela does not diminish the sympathy and high regard some neighbors had for him. For example, the Merlans acknowledged the carver's determination to master his work and granted it, through their patronage, status as art. Thomas Merlan and a few others found that Barela talked about his work all the time.[32] He discussed his personal struggles and family relations, and he conversed with some members of the Anglo art world about his artistic output and intentions. For certain Anglos, Barela provided a rationale, a context, for his artistic goals in a way similar to certain received ideas about Western artists.

Like the Merlans, local Anglo sculptor Ted Egri and his wife, Kit, also had a particularly strong admiration for the carver. However, rather than acquiring many examples of the artist's work for themselves, the couple simply respected it and encouraged its production. When he first met Barela, in the early 1950s, Ted Egri was a painter, recently moved to Taos from Kansas City, where he had taught at the Art Institute. Egri began to sculpt after arriving in New Mexico. Although the stone, metal, and wood sculpture by Egri strongly resembles the wood carvings by Barela, it is difficult to determine whether Barela's abstract forms directly influenced Egri. Nonetheless, a spiritual connection between Egri's affection for Barela's carvings and his own motivation for sculpting is traceable.

A socially conscious artist, originally from New York, Egri developed great sympathy for the wood-carver's social predicament. According to Egri, Barela was "intuitive of humanity. He was aware of human problems through [the experiences of] his own life." But Egri was not interested in Barela because of the carver's association with tradition. In fact, Egri was interested in Barela precisely because of what he saw as a break from the culture of the santero. Egri acknowledges the santos that Barela may have carved early on, but he believed that Barela's abstract pieces were "carvings . . . about people, not about saints." According to Egri, Barela "was not a santero. He was an original carver of human situations, human emotions."

The Egris recognize that their view of Barela certainly differed from that of Barela's own native community. When Barela died, the Egris recall that the Catholic church refused to bury him. Although he had been a religious man, Barela had not followed the rules of the church. And although the carver's daughter cried out for her father at the funeral, Kit recalls that the woman had paid her father little mind when he was alive. The majority of honorary pallbearers at Patrocinio's funeral were Anglo members of the Taos art community.[33]

Barela, Vernon Hunter, and the WPA

Barela is the only resultant mystery following efforts to revive Spanish Colonial arts in New Mexico which did not go far beyond copying old patterns of craft art, furniture, tin candelabra and embroidery.[34]

In 1935, Russell Vernon Hunter (1900–1955), a painter, art teacher, and furniture maker born in Illinois, was appointed director of the Federal Arts Project (FAP) of the Works Progress Administration (WPA) for New Mexico. As state director for the FAP, Hunter worked to create local art projects, solicit sponsors, and select artists for particular activities. His essentially proprietorial role over the arts of New Mexico gave Hunter complete control over the official aesthetic judgment of the state's art.

Although most of the artists who worked for the New Mexico FAP were Anglos trained in a Western fine-art tradition, the FAP, nationally as well as in New Mexico, encouraged the production of regional and local folk arts. The WPA hired Barela, along with other carvers such as Juan Sanchez of Córdova, to produce wood sculpture. Barela began carving in 1931, and from 1936 to 1943 the FAP provided Barela's salary and exhibited his works nationally.

According to some, the FAP years were highly influential in the course of Barela's artistic development. Margaret Berg, Taoseño and life-long friend to Barela, wrote that "during this period he became more creative and broke away from the 'santero' heritage." Barela himself claimed that the "WPA years [were the] best time," because he was then able to devote more time to his carving.[35]

Russell Vernon Hunter's widow, Virginia Hunter Ewing, speaks for many Barela supporters when she remembers the carver as a "folk art 'star'" of the FAP who received national attention.[36] Yet Anglo appreciation of Barela's work was stronger than that for other santeros precisely because of the work's distinction from tradition and elevated status as art. Hunter and others admired Barela not so much because of the santos he made when first inspired to carve, but because the wood-carver stood alone in developing a strong visual style. According to Hunter, "Reproductive work [such as that done by the early-twentieth-century santeros] became copies of copies, finally losing the gouache charm that the early craftsmen made so engaging."[37] E. Boyd also singled out the "original work" of Barela as an example of Hispano wood carving deservedly featured in national exhibits. Distinguishing Barela from other early-twentieth-century santeros, she said, "The deliberate encouragement, without critical reservations, of the poor copying of old santos by Santiago Mata, Juan Sanchez, Emilio Padilla and other artisans has left a long trail of poor stuff behind it into the present."[38]

Because Hunter and others appreciated the aesthetic power of Barela's work apart from its cultural context and association with the santo tradition, they had no language to describe the carvings. Their descriptions of Barela's work had an "orientalizing" flair. For example, Taos poet Wendell Anderson said:

> Many of his carvings have a Moorish ornamentation and flourish: while African forms emerge in many distorted and highly stylized images. One is also reminded of the squat grim idols of the Mexicans and Mayans the Conquistadores found when they arrived in the New World.[39]

Hunter was equally as vague and inarticulate in describing Barela's work: "With the inherent adaptability of his realistic race, he takes things as they are with a fatalism not less than oriental, but he meets them with unconquerable idealism and fortitude."[40] FAP workers and their friends lumped Barela's work together with other non-Western forms, assessing it within elite aesthetic categories reserved for works by members of all non-elite groups.

SPIRITUAL PROTÉGÉS OF BARELA

Since the 1970s, contemporary santeros have taken notice of Barela in a way remarkably similar to the modernist primitivists of the 1930s and 1940s. Although they began their artistry self-consciously, in an effort to construct their own ethnicity, contemporary Hispano wood-carvers celebrate Barela's work for its likeness to that of famous fine artists, and they praise its forms in vague aesthetic terms. They perpetuate an idea of local virtue created by elite members of Anglo culture.

Whereas discussions of Barela's life and work in the 1930s and 1940s were part of a larger exchange about "primitive" art, contemporary santeros' conversations about Barela reflect a local rhetoric about "fine" art. Still, the aesthetic comparisons are the same. Both the early modernists and contemporary santeros draw parallels between Barela's work and work by Henry Moore, Constantin Brancusi, and other artists of the time. Rather than the comparisons themselves, the particular group who makes them changes the value of the rhetoric surrounding the carver. The modernists admired Barela's work for its aesthetic properties, but the reason for the contemporary Hispano wood-carvers' admiration is less clear. Do they celebrate Patrocinio Barela for his talent alone, for the fact that he deviated from the santo tradition, or for the praise that the Anglo modernists bestowed on him?

JOSÉ BENJAMÍN LÓPEZ

José Benjamín López (b. 1947), a santero from the northern New Mexico town of Española, is among those contemporary wood-carvers who have a particularly strong appreciation for Patrocinio Barela. Known especially for his life-size images of the crucifix, carved and painted in a highly expressive manner to depict Christ's suffering, López himself commands a good deal of respect from his carving peers. The expressive nature of López's large carvings, often depicted twisted, in agony, and with much blood, combined with their overwhelming size stand them apart from the more standard replicas of Spanish colonial images that appear with increasing frequency in Santa Fe commercial establishments, public markets, and museums. López's large carvings are neither easy to display in a market context nor charming for visitors unfamiliar with the region. In subject, they are closest to the images used at moradas during Holy Week by members of the Brotherhood of Our Father Jesus. In form, López's large carvings are highly organic, the figures' limbs appearing as natural extensions of the wood.

Since he began carving in 1963, López has maintained a cautious attitude toward the market and museums. Whereas some of his peers, such as Félix López, Eulogio and Zoraida Ortega, Luis Tapia, and Horacio Valdez, have at times entered their works in the Santa Fe Spanish Market, Benjamín López often just visits such markets to see his friends. Through the years, López has sold a few of his pieces to museums and consigned them to galleries, but never in great abundance. López has focused almost exclusively on his work's formal

development and its religious and political significance rather than its economic value. Besides, he views his work as a very personal expression and would rather keep it for his children than sell it.

José Benjamín López is largely responsible for the formation of an informal carving organization called La Escuela Artesana. Translated as the School of Hispano Art and Artists, La Escuela is a group of nine male wood-carvers who united in the 1970s out of a shared need to express themselves in a manner relevant to the experiences of contemporary santeros. Escuela members gather about once a month, usually in the Nambé home of santero Luisito Luján, to share carving techniques and general camaraderie.[41]

La Escuela members have no mentor whose works they copy, but they tend to produce common forms. Along with carving santos, they make unpainted abstract or figurative wood carvings reminiscent of Barela. Some of these carvings take the shape of nude women and men and others have animal forms. Still others are nonrepresentational.

Despite their variations in form, many of these carvings have a twisted quality that reflects the natural course of the wood. In some cases, such as in the abstract carvings of Félix López and Manuel López, they include a variety of different figures in one piece recognizable only by looking at all sides of the object. These pieces especially resemble Barela's figurative work. Félix López, who calls his figurative carvings "moderns," claims that in the early 1980s he began creating his "free-form" carvings "under the influence of Patrocinio Barela."[42] Recalling a trip he once took to Europe, López remembers how he was less inspired by religious statuary he saw in medieval churches than by bronze

sculpture he saw in the Rodin Museum in France. López praises the circularity of Rodin's forms, a quality similar to Barela's sculpture and his own. Not all woodcarvers trace the inspiration of their abstracts to Barela. But they all recognize the Taos carver as a significant aesthetic and spiritual voice in their carving.

José Benjamín López also produces unpainted figurative and nonfigurative sculpture and compares his and Barela's work with elite art, citing Moore, Brancusi, and Picasso as influences; still, he does not necessarily seek validation from the mainstream art world.[43] Unschooled in art, López takes cues from the dominant culture and works independently. In 1980, López, Vicente Martínez, and José Griego y Maestas curated an exhibition of works by Barela. Mounted in a Santa Fe church, the exhibition was an entirely local effort that had a professional presentation. Carefully selecting objects and exhibiting them as rarities in cases and on pedestals, the organizers demonstrated a curatorial finesse highly valued by the elite art world. Nonetheless, because it was not in a museum, the exhibition was intended to provide an unusual opportunity for Hispanos to evaluate for themselves the sculpture of a man whose work had until then largely been the property of Western art enthusiasts.

Lately, López's iconoclasm, like Tapia's, has subsided. Realizing that the sale of his works brings him badly needed income, López is increasingly willing to sell his work to private dealers and nonprofit institutions. He willingly works as a craft demonstrator for museums and public markets.

López's new relationship with the mainstream art world has affected the style of his art. More and more, López produces polychromed santos and animal carvings on a much smaller scale than the large, expressive carvings once considered his trademark. López's animal carvings recall the animal art produced in great abundance for the market by carvers such as Frank Brito, Jr., or the late Felipe Archuleta and his followers.

It has been difficult for the local population to generate a cash income since the very notion was first introduced to New Mexico in the nineteenth century. Those who have historically based their livelihood on local agriculture do not necessarily measure labor in financial terms. López measures labor in terms of craftsmanship, calling himself "an art laborer."[44]

José Benjamín López's view of himself as an artist parallels the feelings he has about Patrocinio Barela. Barela, who worked in sheep and lumber camps and coal mines and potato fields, lived close to the earth. In an essay written for his Barela exhibition, López wrote, Barela "was well acquainted with hard work in the sun all day. . . . He knew the reward of seeing clean rows in the evening, sacks filled with potatoes."[45] According to López, neither he nor Barela separated everyday work from art.

López ranks Barela's work with that of Picasso and Moore, but he also believes that "along with general critical acclaim, Patrocinio's work has . . . influenced the current generation of carvers and sculptors from New Mexico." According to López, "Barela's work relates to the working person because he was a working man, a laborer and migrant farm worker." Therefore, "it is the responsibility of the Chicano artist working today to follow Patrocinio's example."

José Benjamín López takes ownership of the fine-art categories he applies to Barela's work. According to López, "Picasso drew inspiration from Africa, [but] Barela drew inspiration from his heart. . . . He applied his [own] experiences to his carvings." Barela's "carvings were a conveyance of feeling, . . . [with] Barela growing out of the wood, [and] the wood growing out of Barela."[46]

Fig. 62. Large Cristo, ca. 1979, by José Benjamín López. 154" x 140" x 14 1/2". Until 1992, when this Cristo was moved to the Gene Autry Western Heritage Museum, it was located outside, in Jose Benjamín and Irene López's front yard. José Benjamin originally intended the piece to be unpainted. He applied the white paint, now peeling, to protect the piece from the elements. Courtesy José Benjamín and Irene López. Collection: Gene Autry Western Heritage Museum. Photo: Mary Peck.

< **Fig. 63.** Large Cristo (detail), ca. 1979, by José Benjamín López. Courtesy José Benjamín and Irene López. Collection: Gene Autry Western Heritage Museum. Photo: Mary Peck.

According to López and others such as Ted Egri, the faces Barela carved were not taken from anonymous sculpture made in exotic places; they were faces representing everyday people.

López's discussion of himself and Patrocinio Barela is local, political, and Chicano. Although López values fine art over all other types of artistic expression, he gives this elite form roots in the New Mexican soil. Rather than place Barela's works in an original or "authentic" past created by the hegemony, López recalls Barela in terms of his own ethnic memory, his own personal and cultural experience. He invents Barela in his own image, as an artist sprung directly from Mother Earth. In so doing, he can then argue, "We do not need societies dictating what our art should be."

LUIS BARELA, JR.

Luis Barela, Jr., is Patrocinio Barela's grandson. Born in 1961, only three years before Barela died, the younger Barela never saw his grandfather carve. Still, the young Barela attributes his interest and skill to Barela. According to Luis, the 1980 exhibition of Patrocinio's work "really opened [his] eyes [to carving]." "When I first started carving," he explains to a newspaper interviewer, "I had a strong feeling, with my first piece, that my grandfather was encouraging me to carve."[47] When he first saw the Barela show, Luis was on his way to the Albuquerque Technical-Vocational Institute to train as a diesel mechanic. However, ten years later, with a family in tow, Barela, Jr., returned to Talpa, where he grew up, to pursue a carving occupation.

Fig. 64. Interior, Luisito Luján's house, Nambé, 1992. Unfinished santo with gesso, by Luisito Luján. Courtesy Luisito Luján. Photo: Mary Peck.

Fig. 65. Mermaid, n.d., by José Benjamín López. Collection of the artist. Photo: Mary Peck.

OVERLEAF

Left

Fig. 66. Nicho, 1991, and abstract wood carving, ca. 1980s, by Félix López. Collection of the artist. Photo: Mary Peck.

Right

Fig. 67. Bulto of San Antonio (Saint Anthony), 1991, by José Benjamín López, aspen, cottonwood root, and natural pigments. Collection: Gene Autry Western Heritage Museum. Photo: Susan Einstein.

As a boy, Barela, Jr., had little opportunity to see his grandfather's carvings. The carver's family never thought to save Barela's sculpture, and through the years, examples of the works remained unavailable to them. Today, in retrospect, family members regret that they do not own a private collection. Luis Barela, Sr., explains that Remedios, his mother and Patrocinio's wife, did not understand her husband's carving. "Even my wife," Barela, Sr., continues, "she wasn't interested in that [wood carving], but now that she knows the value of it, but it's too late." Even with their recent interest in Barela's work, family members have only been able to acquire examples through purchase or trade.

The value of Patrocinio Barela's sculpture is economic, originally dictated by an Anglo elite. Although pure profit motivation does not necessarily characterize Hispano American attitudes toward personal ownership, of land or other possessions, it made little sense for the Barela family to ignore the benefits of acquiring their relative's work.[48] Because of their new interest in Patrocinio Barela's wood carvings and Luis Barela, Jr.'s sculpture done in the style of his grandfather, the Barela family has achieved recognition from the Anglo art world. They have also entered into a new social stratum. Still, the family incorporates the Anglo elite appreciation of Barela carvings into their daily lives with a larger goal of staying together as a family and asserting, to some extent, their ethnic separation from the Anglo community.

Luis Barela, Jr., first presented his carvings to the public in 1990, at Spanish Market. Although the young Barela entered the contemporary section of the market, his works represented a nod toward tradition, or what folklorist John Dorst calls a simulated continuity with the past, similar to the endless

reproductions of Spanish colonial santos in the traditional section.[49] Barela makes his carvings from juniper, just like his grandfather did, and explores corresponding philosophical themes of family, religion, and nature in figurative and abstract forms. In the market context, the young Barela's carvings represent a fixed image of his grandfather that the largely Anglo patrons can value and will ultimately buy.

Metaphorically, Barela, Jr.'s carvings echo a four-color poster of Patrocinio that Chicano artist and activist Edward González also sold in the contemporary section of Spanish Market. The poster, which depicts Patrocinio holding a carving at his feet and sitting in a chair that has a Rio Grande blanket folded over it, frames the carver in a context of tradition and advertises him in an art show format. The poster reproduces an oil painting by González that was itself copied from a black-and-white poster originally produced for the 1980 Barela show.

The original Barela show poster is prized by contemporary carvers who display it in their homes. Through the years, the Barela poster has come to signify such a strong idea of ethnic liberation and free artistic expression that actual carvings by Patrocinio need not be available at market for Barela to be bought and sold. Barela posters and Luis Barela, Jr., wood carvings dematerialize and reproduce in print and wood the carvings of Patrocinio. They literally reflect themselves. But in so doing, they risk dissolving into an endless series of references to references, losing claims to personal or cultural ownership.

Ironically, Luis Barela, Jr., saved his carvings and, by extension, González's posters from such a dissolution. He set up his carvings in a market booth, but he did not offer many of them for sale. Not wanting to repeat what happened to his grandfather's carvings (none of his relatives owned his work), the young wood-carver made carvings for various family members. His first priority was to establish himself as a carver among his kin. Luis Barela, Jr., incorporated the artistic preferences of the market but did not become totally absorbed by them. He reproduced a style that may have at first been appreciated by the elite Anglo art world, but he reclaimed his grandfather as his aesthetic as well as genetic forebear.

LEO SALAZAR

Although most wood-carvers who talk about Barela did not know the man personally, at least one santero spoke of Barela in more intimate terms. Leo Salazar of Taos (1934–91) claimed that when he was a young man he apprenticed with Patrocinio Barela. Salazar talked with pride about the tools he acquired from Barela's woodshed after he died, and how after that he "traced Barela's work for a year."

Like Luis Barela, Jr., Salazar followed Barela's style. He carved a big nose, deep eyes and slits for the mouth and eyes of a figure, with "just a little cut at the [lid]," and he left other body parts, such as hands, unarticulated. Salazar also copied Barela's marketing techniques. He visited Anglo supporters of Barela's and called local galleries, "just like Barela did."[50] Enamored not only of Barela's style, Salazar was impressed with the Anglo recognition, or at least remuneration, the master received.

Although Salazar considered himself a protégé of Barela, he also claimed to be a self-taught wood-carver. The Taos art community did not value replication of another artist's work. To make a transition from copying Barela to developing an individual style, Salazar began producing religious images. Like Barela, Salazar continued to work with juniper, but he eventually built up his own santo

Fig. 68. *Baboon,* n.d., by Leroy Archuleta, wood, rope, glass marbles, 25 1/4" x 22" x 13". Collection: Gene Autry Western Heritage Museum. Gift of Robert and Ruth Vogele. Photo: Susan Einstein.

Fig. 69. Barela family members, Talpa, 1992. Top row (left to right): Luis Barela, Jr., Trinnie Barela, Christine Vigil. Middle row: Angelica Barela, Alicia Barela. Bottom row: Eric Barela, Robert Barela, Daniel Barela. The Barela family poses in front of the new adobe house Barela, Jr., built on family land next to his parents' house. Barela, Jr., chose the labor-intensive method of adobe construction over an easier process such as building in frame because he wanted to recreate the historic house style of the region. Barela, Jr.'s building choice was based on economics as well as aesthetics. In Talpa, as in many places throughout New Mexico, adobe structures have more real estate value than other modern building types. Photo: Mary Peck.

Fig. 70. Luis Barela, Jr., in his booth at 1991 Spanish Market. Photo: Miguel A. Gandert.

repertoire, including about forty different saints, "woman saints, man saints." He learned about saints' attributes from patrons' suggestions, not through his own religious beliefs or his family.[51]

Just before he died, Salazar printed a pamphlet about his work. The pamphlet included a map to Salazar's house, his address and phone number, black-and-white photographs of some images, a picture of Salazar himself, and a paragraph about his work. The pamphlet was available at Salazar's Spanish Market table. Placed amidst a repetitive myriad of santos, the pamphlets represented not only the carvings for sale but their abundant availability. Although more sophisticated than Barela's random and often desperate visits to sympathetic neighbors and collectors, Salazar's marketing technique was based on an idea of Barela as innovative wood-carver and participant in the fine-art world. For Salazar, the activity of selling blended with the history of Barela as he experienced it, which included art patronage.

An Emergent Reconsideration

Contemporary santeros regard free expression and self-legitimacy, so crucial to the Chicano cause, as by-products of the fame Barela achieved in his own day. Ironically, the language that describes Barela's work is the same as it was in the 1930s; only the people who use it are different, and the adjectives are reversed. Whereas the early modernists talked about Barela in terms of primitivism, contemporary Hispano wood-carvers link Barela with modernism. They transfer their political ideology to Barela and select the tenet of "truth to materials" as a means of aesthetic exploration and, in some cases, economic reward.

Although at least one carver, Luis Tapia, acknowledges the datedness of the historic moment during which Barela carved, he also excuses it by claiming that "Barela was ahead of his time." Tapia further defends Barela by challenging opinions about his alcoholism. "Barela's style was so good and so consistent that it was hard to believe he was a drunk," Tapia says. "If Barela was intoxicated all the time, how would he be able to produce such finely styled pieces?"

Still, as Tapia explains away claims against Barela, he critiques him from an elite art perspective. Distancing himself from the cultural and political attention that contemporary wood-carvers give Barela, Tapia wonders if the quality of Barela's work has been overrated. A savvy participant in the Santa Fe gallery scene, Tapia also considers that "Barela's prolific output may have [ultimately] been a detriment" to him. For example, Dewey Galleries had some pieces for sale and they couldn't sell them." This reevaluation, so steeped in contemporary art-world debates about the value of art versus its salability, may at first glance seem contradictory to the unflinching praise Tapia and his colleagues bestow on Barela. Because, however, much of the admiration of Barela's work centers on features that first caught public interest through trained Anglo artists, Tapia's critique reflects an ultimate power—to oppose a Western-derived commendation of local art on its own terms.

Fig. 71. The Barela, Jr., family living room, Talpa, 1992. National Association of Chicano Studies poster of Patrocinio Barela by Edward M. Gonzalez. Wood carvings by Patrocinio Barela and Luis Barela, Jr., Courtesy: Luis Barela, Jr. Photo: Mary Peck.

Fig. 72. Leo Salazar, 1990 Spanish Market.
Photo: Laurie Beth Kalb.

3

SPANISH COLONIAL REPLICAS BY OVIEDO CARVINGS AND BRONZE

IN THE VILLAGE OF CHIMAYÓ, approximately thirty-five miles north by northeast of Santa Fe, lies the home of Marco and Patricia Oviedo and their family. On top of a hill that rises directly from New Mexico's Route 76, the house faces a road that provides thousands of tourists each year with an ephemeral view of Hispano village culture.[1] The Oviedo home lies between the renowned pilgrimage church, the Santuario de Chimayó, located in one of the village's two plazas, and the wood-carving community of Córdova, made famous because of successful social and economic interactions between outside visitors and village craftspeople. The house is in a section of Chimayó called La Centinela, meaning "sentinel" or "outpost" in English. A few miles from the santuario, La Centinela is occupied mostly by members of the Trujillo family. Patricia A. Trujillo-Oviedo, Marco's wife, descends from a Hispano New Mexican family who settled the area in the early eighteenth century, irrigating and farming the land. Today, the area remains largely a Trujillo outpost.

The Oviedos make their home comfortable for the family and inviting for the recreational visitor. Along with selling santos, the Oviedos sell donkey rides and arrange elaborate displays of the materials and tools involved in producing religious images. Recently, they have turned their two-car garage into an art gallery where visitors can view their work. Like the santuario, the village of Córdova, and many other Chimayó establishments, the Oviedos' home has become a "must" stop in the art cartography of northern New Mexico.

In making santos, the Oviedos replicate Spanish colonial religious imagery. They pride themselves on their ability to produce replicas of eighteenth-

and nineteenth-century santos. In choosing donkeys as animals for riding, they also recall beasts of burden used in the colonial era. Their home, a two-story adobe structure with pitched metal roof, upstairs *balcón* (balcony), and first floor *portal* (arcade), resembles Spanish colonial architecture from the late-nineteenth-century territorial period. Together, these fragments of Spanish colonial life set the stage for a type of "museumized" residence, a sort of living history exhibit where tourists and other visitors can gain a sense of an idea of daily life from a bygone era. Providing visitors with a glimpse of historic architecture, farming, and santos, the Oviedos offer an entire packaged tour, a representation of the past they wish to sell, albeit in a newly constructed site that also includes an art gallery.

This chapter explores the way one family of santeros participates in the past by manipulating the present. By creating "an extended ethnographic theme park," the Oviedos manage authenticity by basing their production more on the demands of the present and on the marketplace than on any real personal experience of Spanish colonial life.[2] Although much work has been done on the way museums fragment culture in their attempts to represent it, less has been said about the way members of cultures ordinarily put on ethnographic display perform themselves.[3] Marco and Patricia Oviedo use dominant forms of ethnographic and aesthetic display for commercial purposes, appropriating santo making for themselves. They both participate in and subvert the dominant culture as a means of inventing their own traditional identity. To discuss the Oviedos' wood carvings and other events at their home is necessarily to feature both Marco and Patricia as producers and sellers; however, their sense of tradition, continuity, and business is largely shaped by Marco. So I turn first to him.

Fig. 73. Marco and Patricia Oviedo's neoterritorial style home, Chimayó, built 1985. Courtesy Marco and Patricia Oviedo. Photo: Mary Peck, 1991.

Fig. 74. Marco and Patricia Oviedo in their living
room, Chimayó, 1992. Photo: Mary Peck.

Marco Oviedo was born in 1948 in Mexico City. He was raised and educated in Spain, France, and Mexico City before moving to Las Cruces, New Mexico, in 1978. Holding two bachelor of science and two master of science degrees, Oviedo came to Las Cruces to work on a doctorate in animal sciences at New Mexico State University. There he met and married Patricia A. Trujillo of Chimayó, who was also pursuing graduate courses at New Mexico State. Oviedo has four children, Oliver J., Daisy Annette, and Marco Antonio II (Tony), from a previous marriage, and Jacobo Javier (J. J.) from his marriage with Patricia. All four children live with Marco and Patricia in Chimayó. Oviedo's mother, Angélica López Oviedo, spends winters with the family. Marco and Patricia must work hard to support their large family.

Although the Oviedos lived in Las Cruces until 1985, Marco began wood carving in the 1970s, while working on his doctorate. In fact, one year, when Oviedo lost a graduate assistantship from his university, he and his wife set up a wood-carving business in Las Cruces, calling it Old World Arts. A commercial enterprise advertised using the language of preservation, of "conserving the ancient art of carpentry from the time of our ancestors," the family business produced handmade wooden signs, furniture, and Spanish colonial ornamental wood carvings.

Along with his furniture for Old World Arts, Oviedo made santos and animal carvings for the Santa Fe Spanish Market. Although he was not born into a Hispano New Mexican family, generally a criterion for acceptance as a Spanish Market participant, market officials welcomed Oviedo into their ranks. When he first entered the market, Oviedo, like Luis Tapia, was one among a very few santeros who participated at all.

Oviedo learned many technical and marketing skills by conducting his own museum and library research, and from members of the Anglo art world, among them the late Alan Vedder, whom he considered a "second father." Unlike some self-conscious wood-carvers, Oviedo speaks quite favorably of the Spanish Market, its possibilities, and even its Anglo officers. He even endorses the SCAS's power to determine the traditional quality of the art submitted for the market and the separation between a traditional market on the plaza and a contemporary one. In Oviedo's words,

> The Spanish Market is such an important event. E. Boyd is the mother of the *renacimiento* (revival) of the Spanish Culture. Bill Field, Bud Redding, Alan Vedder, E. Boyd.[4] They make a good effort at distinguishing contemporary from traditional art. If I came to look at art from Tibet, I don't know anything about art from Tibet, I would appreciate a distinction between contemporary and traditional.

Since 1979, when they began participating in Spanish Market, the Oviedos have won seven awards for excellence from the Spanish Colonial Arts Society.

Despite significant encouragement and success with Anglo aficionados, Oviedo credits his family for providing him with the proper knowledge and birthright to practice wood carving. Claiming to be an eighth-generation member of a family whose wood carving reaches back to eighteenth-century Oviedo, Spain, he argues:

Fig. 75. Bulto of San Agustín (Saint Augustine), ca. 1980s, by Marco and Patricia Oviedo. Photo: Richard D. Wickstrom.

[The production of santos] is not really New Mexican art. It's Mexican art. When people were producing santos here in the seventeenth, eighteenth, and nineteenth centuries, it was Spanish. But, I'm not going to make a big deal. The beauty of this is I don't compete with anybody. In my style, I don't compete with anybody.

He further explains that his grandfather, who was an accountant in Spain, also produced saints for churches and individuals. Oviedo also owns a book written by a great uncle that includes drawings of anatomy and recipes for making natural dyes. Although he only recently acquired this book from his father, an agricultural engineer in Mexico City, and the book itself contains a lot of scientific technical detail, Oviedo maintains that it has been valuable to him as a reference for making pigments and carving santos.

Oviedo had to convince his father to give him the book. His father insisted that the book not be commercialized. In other words, Oviedo's father did not want his relative's document associated with "buying and selling," or "work[ing] cheap." Oviedo contrasts these attitudes with being an artist. He distinguishes between commercialism and the production of traditional art, but he practices both:

> I don't buy and sell. My obligation is to keep the tradition [that is] from behind and to keep it for the future. . . . I'm here to be an artist, . . . and try to pass the tradition on to my kids.

For Oviedo, as for all contemporary santeros, the way to perpetuate tradition is to market it.

FAMILY

Marco Oviedo's invocation of tradition derives primarily from his mentors in the museum and art patronage worlds and from his ancestors. Patricia's family might be a third component. Patricia A. Trujillo-Oviedo descends from a family that claims a history of more than 250 years of weaving. Throughout the Spanish colonial period, many Chimayó villagers established themselves as skillful and prosperous weavers. Government officials in Mexico City believed that weaving, along with increased commerce in hides, animals, and produce, would improve economic conditions on the northern frontier. A contract was formulated to send the expert craftsmen and brothers Ignacio Ricardo and Juan Bazán to live in Santa Fe and teach the weaving trade to the area's youth.[5] Chimayó weavers were almost exclusively men. For the most part, they either worked for or were members of two prominent Chimayó weaving families, the Ortegas or the Trujillos. Through the years, those two families became joined through marriages.[6]

Patricia's father, Jacobo Trujillo (1911–90), was among the most famous and financially successful of the Trujillo weavers. After retiring from thirty years as a property manager at Los Alamos National Laboratory, Mr. Trujillo came back to Chimayó to run a weaving business in a way that his forebears did. He learned how to weave from his mother, Francisquita Ortega Trujillo, and he passed along his weaving skills to his son, Irvin, and his daughter-in-law, Lisa. Although at first he sold his weavings from his house, Trujillo eventually con-

Fig. 76. The Trujillos' booth at 1991 Spanish Market. Irvin Trujillo in foreground, Lisa Trujillo and Jacobo's widow, Isabelle Trujillo, in background. Photo: Miguel A. Gandert.

verted a garage into a weaving shop he called Centinela Traditional Arts. He sold his own weavings and those by other craftspeople.

Unlike his late father-in-law, Marco Oviedo sells only images he and his immediate family create. Despite the difference in their business practices, Oviedo holds Jacobo Trujillo in a sort of traditional esteem. He credits Trujillo with teaching him a great deal about premodern New Mexico. Oviedo affirms his own relationship to New Mexico tradition through his relationship with the master weaver. Oviedo claims that "Jake helped [me] a lot." He was a "guy with a bunch of vision." For Marco, Jacobo's vision was both financial and creative. In his shop, Trujillo displayed Oviedo's santos and animal carvings as well as blankets by his son and daughter-in-law. This business arrangement gave Oviedo the right to participate in the region's traditions.

Although Oviedo links his wood carving to his Mexican and Spanish roots, he replicates northern New Mexico colonial santos. And he has made his home in Chimayó. At least part of the reason for settling in Chimayó was Patricia's desire to move back to her hometown after seventeen years away. Although she still works in Santa Fe and Los Alamos, she and Marco have worked hard to reconstruct a rural life for themselves in Chimayó.

Patricia Oviedo's love for horses, the availability of her family's land for corrals, her husband's broad knowledge of agricultural animals, and their desire to succeed financially in the economically depressed Santa Cruz river valley led the Oviedos to establish a business called Paseo de la Tierra Vieja, Ltd. (roughly, Ride of the Old Land). They bought a variety of breeds of donkeys and sold rides to tourists. The animal business and occasional sale of santos from Trujillo's shop provided revenues; the Oviedo family settled into Chimayó village life. In 1985, the couple and their youngest son moved to a seven-acre piece of property that Patricia inherited. It is this land, which presently holds a growing number of animal stalls, a barn and storage building, a garage and hayloft, an arena, and the art gallery attached to the house, that the Oviedos open up to a visiting public. Although the Oviedos do not charge admission to their site, an abundance of directional signs in English and separate entrances for visitors to the art gallery mark it as a theme park, a place where local traditions are set up for viewing.

AUTHENTICITY

Just as the northern New Mexico present is in many ways shaped and defined by representations of the past, the Oviedos' participation in the past is dictated by contemporary expectations and needs. They seem given to shaping and viewing their present reality as the natural unfolding from a definitively significant past.[7] The Spanish colonial santos they replicate, the legacy they invoke from their ancestors, Anglo mentors, patrons and friends, and the crafts they produce in their home are all practiced under the rubric of authenticity, of something absolutely true to its original source. Authenticity, however, in northern New Mexico, is a highly commodified term. For more than a hundred years, the notion of an essential, bounded tradition has been packaged and sold to tourists in the form of Rio Grande blankets, Indian pottery and kachinas, and other material fragments of native life.

The Oviedos' efforts at representing Hispano cultural authenticity to outside visitors may illustrate the integration of tourism into daily life. Yet it is precisely the Oviedos' reinvention of Spanish colonial santos and public display of tradition, their version of an inherited culture, that has deep roots in local history. To understand the source of the Oviedo enterprise, I offer a brief ethnography of tourism and the presentation of tradition in Chimayó. This can provide a deeper comprehension not only of authenticity but also of the process of authentification, and of how the Oviedos render their representations of tradition authoritative.

CHIMAYÓ

The weavers of Chimayó boast a bustling village industry. Although the materials used to make Chimayó blankets have changed, from hand-spun, vegetal-dyed wools to manufactured, synthetic-dyed yarns, the business of producing them remains the same. Throughout the twentieth century, Chimayó blankets, like wood carvings from Córdova, have represented for tourists a tangible piece of New Mexico history. Like the Córdova wood carvings, Chimayó blankets act as mediators between local Hispanos and visiting Anglos. [8]

More than objects that represent negotiations between tourists and villagers, Chimayó blankets are tied to preservation, commodification, education, and the aesthetics that craftspeople present to visitors. For example, local billboards and signs painted directly onto the facade of Ortega's Weaving Shop assert that the enterprise reaches back eight generations. Shop owner David Ortega often wears a handsome vest pieced together from Chimayó weavings and is happy to point interested visitors toward the loom room, where some of the Ortega weaving happens.

Irvin and Lisa Trujillo operate Centinela Traditional Arts. Recently, they built a large, airy showroom attached to the old shop. This new room contrasts with the store's original section, where visitors walked into a cramped space and had to flip through a rack to see the textiles. Today, visitors enter a veritable gallery, where each of the couple's rugs and blankets hangs on the wall individually. Each weaving has a label, noting its style and price. The showroom's door, walls, and floor are rough-hewn local pine. Like the textiles for sale, the showroom has a handmade look. The entire enterprise resembles a museum. Jacobo Trujillo's weavings, once offered for sale but now covetously collected by his family, are now permanently displayed in the store's old section, where the shop is outmoded.

Chimayó has exhibited more than its textiles. It has done the same with religion. One of the village's two plazas, El Potrero, is bounded by two churches, La Capilla del Santo Niño de Atocha and the pilgrimage shrine of Nuestro Señor de Esquípulas, also called El Santuario de Chimayó. Although both churches were originally private chapels, only La Capilla del Santo Niño de Atocha remains in family hands. El Santuario de Chimayó, built in 1816, was purchased anonymously in 1929, thanks to Mary Austin's efforts to save it from being sold piecemeal by family owners who could no longer maintain it. Once the building was purchased, it was turned over to the Spanish Colonial Arts Society, who held it "in trust . . . for worship and as a religious museum."[9]

Today, while the church continues to function as a pilgrimage site, busloads of tourists as well as devout Catholics from surrounding Hispano settlements visit El Santuario de Chimayó. The church is now both a historic shrine and a religious center that combines religious and commercial activities. Clearly

Fig. 77. Potrero Trading Post. La Capilla del
Santo Niño de Atocha (Chapel of the Holy Child
of Atocha) in background, El Potrero Plaza,
Chimayó, 1991. Courtesy Raymond Bal and
Susana Duran. Photo: Mary Peck.

defined land boundaries, sidewalks, and parking spaces make the building accessible to visitors. Gift shops have opened, and a priest is now generally available to anyone who asks for one.[10] A bronze plaque designates the santuario a national historic landmark, and a church brochure advertises it as the "Lourdes of America." The church's healing room appears on picture postcards. Plexiglass encases three of the sanctuary's santos. Just as the santos are sealed behind protective material, so is a particular perspective. Religion and the spiritual life are marked off from the background of poverty and violence experienced by many santuario parishioners. Lifted out of its local context for nonparishioners, the church achieves a kind of historic value that has little to do with its surrounding community. Rather, it is mapped out on a tourist route.

Adjacent to El Potrero plaza, Rancho de Chimayó Restaurant has been in business for twenty-seven years. It serves local fare, such as enchiladas, tacos, burritos, sopaipillas, and flan. Owned by the Jaramillo family, one of the earliest Spanish families to settle in Chimayó, the restaurant serves both a local clientele and a great many tourists. Situated against lush green meadows where horses once grazed, the restaurant offers a picturesque setting. It is a convenient stop after a visit to the santuario and El Potrero. The parking lot of Rancho de Chimayó is large enough to accommodate tour buses, and the menus are in Spanish and English. Framed photographs of the works of local craftspeople, most notably the carvings of Marco and Patricia Oviedo, hang in each of the restaurant's rooms. The Oviedos are among the Jaramillos' most frequent customers, entertaining out-of-town friends at "the Rancho."

The Rancho, Ortegas' Weaving Shop, Centinela Ranch, El Santuario de Chimayó, and other establishments individually and collectively transform Chimayó into a living exhibit. Everyday practices such as those associated with food, craftsmanship, and religion are set up for formal viewing and tasting, becoming what Barbara Kirshenblatt-Gimblett calls "quotidian dramas," in which one person's life is another person's spectacle.[11]

THE OVIEDO HOME

The combined wood-carving and business skills that the Oviedos honed in Las Cruces, where they ran Old World Arts, fit well with the exhibiting and commercial orientations of Chimayó. The promotional flyer for Old World Arts reads, "Everything in Woodworking. . . . Old World Arts is at your service with the patience and quality of yesteryear": the past is at our service at the Oviedos' home in Chimayó. It is there as we want it—for our enjoyment, edification, and, ultimately, for our consumption. The Oviedo home is arranged so that it provides the opportunity for us to possess an image of the past.

Billboards and cardboard markers abound in Chimayó and nearby Córdova, beckoning visitors to many commercial establishments. The Oviedos, who invite visitors into their home with signs, are no exception to the local advertising rule. Two professionally printed billboards along the stretch of Route 76 that leads to their house mark the Oviedo site. In the spaces on their property where they welcome visitors, the Oviedos place directional signs every twenty or so feet. The mailbox and the driveway sport handmade markers that read Oviedos and Visitors Welcome, respectively. A yellow diamond-shaped marker resembling a highway traffic sign reads Donkeys Xing, with a picture of two adult burros and a baby burro. On the side of a stall, a small sign warns, "Don't

Fig. 78. Billboard and mailbox marker for Oviedo Carvings, Chimayó, 1991. Courtesy Marco and Patricia Oviedo. Photo: Mary Peck.

Fig. 79. Oviedo donkey stalls and signs cautioning visitors about animals, Chimayó, 1991. Courtesy Marco and Patricia Oviedo. Photo: Mary Peck.

Fig. 80. Tack room with red cloth trade banner for Oviedo Carvings, Chimayó, 1991. Courtesy Marco and Patricia Oviedo. Photo: Mary Peck.

Fig. 81. Sign and arena for Burro Trail Rides, Oviedo home site, Chimayó, 1991. Courtesy Marco and Patricia Oviedo. Photo: Mary Peck.

Fig. 82. *Noah's Ark*, signed by Marco A. Oviedo,
1989. Collection: Gene Autry Western Heritage
Museum. Donative purchase from Robert and
Ruth Vogele. Photo: Susan Einstein.

< **Fig. 83.** *Noah's Ark* (detail), 1989, by Marco
Oviedo. Collection: Gene Autry Western Heritage
Museum. Donative purchase from Robert and
Ruth Vogele. Photo: Susan Einstein.

feed your fingers to the donkeys." A red cloth banner hanging on the exterior of the tack room says, Welcome to Oviedo Carvings. A Family of Carvers Since 1737.

Signs at the Oviedos propel a sense of location on visitors and contribute to their sense of being looked at.[12] As he parodies directional signs that warn against hurting animals or children, Oviedo creates new markers that caution visitors against hurting mules, donkeys, or themselves. All the signs are in English. Their designs, such as the yellow "highway marker," are familiar to travelers from anywhere. The red welcome banner sports the same sort of language as the sign for the Ortegas' Weaving Shop located down the road, which reads, Ortegas' Weaving Shop. Eight Generations of Weaving. The inscriptions on the Ortegas' and the Oviedos' signs suggest family continuity and tradition; their plaques designate a location for the idea. As markers for tourists, the signs themselves are objects that let visitors know they are in friendly (or at least safe) territory.[13]

Only nine years old, the Oviedo home could be considered the antithesis of antiquity. Nevertheless, its signs celebrate the past. The Oviedo establishment is historically memorable not because of what it is, but because of what it resembles.[14]

An overall theme permeates the events and artifacts that the Oviedos present to visitors. This theme centers on a story told by Marco, who claims, "The way I see myself here is like a farmer, as in the old times. You need to take care of your plants, animals. I'm mostly an animal person. I take care of animals—goats, chickens, cows, pigeons, donkeys, horses." As Oviedo further explains, Spanish colonial santeros did more than carve religious images. They, too, had to work their land.

Through their business, Paseo de la Tierra Vieja, Ltd., the Oviedos claim that their lives represent traditional Hispano life. They plan their business with creativity and precision, with the animals forming an integral part of their public display. The couple chose donkeys over horses for their trail rides because, according to Patricia, "donkeys would be something different. Besides, they fit with the history of the area." As beasts of burden used by Spanish colonists, donkeys are "authentic." As an "off-beat" type of animal used for leisure rides, donkeys have a marketable edge. Finally, because donkeys are difficult to breed, Marco could tap his expertise in animal sciences.

The Oviedos' donkeys also recall Spanish colonial New Mexico Catholicism. According to Patricia, riding a donkey is "like riding through 300 years of history. . . . The best way to see this 'old land' is from one of the oldest perspectives, from the back of a donkey. The standard donkey originated in northern Africa . . . and came with Columbus on his second voyage in 1493." Further, Patricia explains, "the donkey is the chosen animal of Christ," referring to the use of the beast in biblical times, and the so-called Jesus Cross, the transverse stripe on the burro's back.[15]

Patricia Oviedo takes responsibility for taking out trail riders. She carefully maps out her burro rides. The rides themselves contribute to the notion of New Mexico as America's Orient. She takes trail riders up a path to the top of a high ridge on the Centinela Ranch, pointing out eroded mesas, arroyos (dry brooks) where members of the Brotherhood of Our Father Jesus have practiced Holy Week rituals, and prehistoric Indian gardens located on Bureau of Land Management land. On one burro ride I took with Patricia and her son J. J., the boy turned to me and said, "It's just like Egypt."

The burro trail ride not only provides the visitor with a bit of Spanish colonialism but also combines Spanish colonialism with recreation. The trail rides of Paseo de la Tierra Vieja consist of what Kirshenblatt-Gimblett calls "the major tropes of ethnographic display, from the perspective of the tourist industry—the promise of visual penetration, access to the back region of other people's lives, the life world of others as our playground, and the view that people are most themselves when at play."[16]

As Patricia anticipates her visitors' every expectation, she does so reflexively. For example, shortly before I took a burro ride, Patricia explained how she guides her trail riders and what she might offer in my case. She said, "And if you get me in the right mood, I might even tell you about the history of the region and show you the bones of the cowasaurus rex and the bovidactyl." I, bleary-eyed from a day's field work, responded excitedly, "Oh, really?" Patricia then laughed and said, "You'd probably believe all this." She repeated the words *cowasaurus rex* a couple of times, and I finally realized she was making a joke. Oviedo made up the words *cowasaurus* and *bovidactyl* by combining names for agricultural animals with suffixes for dinosaurs. By adding prefixes that stood for cattle, Patricia made a joke about the nature of exploration and discovery that leisure tours such as her burro rides were meant to elicit. By turning dinosaurs into a species of cattle, or vice versa, Patricia personalized, or domesticated, the old bones and sites her tourists passed, demystifying and making a joke of something held sacred. In her mild ridicule of the tourist *and* me, Patricia reversed her role from one who is observed to one who observes.

The establishment of Paseo de la Tierra Vieja is simply that—an establishment, a representation of two people's notions of who they would like to be. It is a pastiche of cultural and personal experiences and influences as well as local conveniences that combine to form a type of recreational facility that integrates well into Chimayó. Although they feature donkeys, traditional agricultural animals, for the trail ride, the trail ride itself is as much a part of tradition as anything else. In twentieth-century Chimayó, the business of tourism, or the creation of leisure for outside visitors, has been passed down through the generations perhaps more so than the reliance on the donkey as a beast of burden. Although there may have been no trail rides per se in Chimayó before Paseo de la Tierra Vieja, certainly animal rides are a common component of adult as well as children's activities offered at zoos, nature preserves, and national parks—other places that tourists to Chimayó are apt to go.

Since acquiring donkeys in 1983, the Oviedos have developed their jackstock holdings into a bustling, lucrative, and sophisticated business. Along with offering trail rides to visitors, the Oviedos buy, breed, and sell a wide variety of donkeys. The many breeds recall a broad range of animal figures Marco carved early in his career. Working in exotic hardwoods, Oviedo produced small, intricate carvings of a great variety of creatures. Unlike the jackstock sales, the animal carvings were not economical. They required a lot of time to produce and were small, not bringing in much money. This was why the Oviedos changed their carving repertoire from animals to santos.

The Oviedos' sales of live burro rides resembles what some locals skeptically call "coyote art," available in galleries and gift shops in Santa Fe, Chimayó, and Taos. Like the donkey, the coyote, and, to a lesser extent, rabbits, trout, snakes, various birds, and other animals, have been marketed and accepted by the consumer, critic, dealer, museum professional, and folk art aficionado as emblematic of New Mexico. Charles Briggs quotes one writer as saying, "The carving of ani-

mal figures is a natural outgrowth of lifestyles here."[17]

The general attitude toward folk art animals parallels that which Patricia Oviedo claims for her living burros: "They fit with the history of the area." But in the late twentieth century, the history of the area is often simply a packaged ideal, or in the case of the burro rides, a packaged tour. The meaning and significance of the past have been greatly affected by the very commemoration of them.[18] Moreover, commemoration, or tradition, as a tangible commodity that can pay family bills, distances history and "native life-styles" from themselves even further. Not only trail rides and wood carvings, but t-shirts, mugs, posters, and note cards bear the imprint and the design of "native," "historic" New Mexican creatures. In contemporary New Mexico, animal carvings and other souvenirs become *hyperreal*, to use semiotician Umberto Eco's term.[19] They become fake copies of an imagined ideal.

Like the selection of donkeys for trail rides, the Oviedo home reflects the couple's ideal of a preindustrial, rural way of life. Oviedo, who is a self-proclaimed "enemy of mobile homes," built his home of eighteen-inch-thick adobe bricks. "I needed [my house] to be like the old houses," he says. And, he recalls, "[old] Spanish houses around here have a little balcón." Oviedo believes that the newer prefab houses are taking away the beauty of the region.

To learn how to build in adobe, Oviedo did not approach members of the local community. Rather, he took a class in adobe construction while at New Mexico State University. "We carried vigas to Las Cruces and back to Chimayó. We love the land the way it is. . . . We're not putting [on] any front here," Oviedo has said. Oviedo aligns authenticity and tradition with a sort of handmade purity from a bygone era. No matter that the local community has little connection to such a source and that mobile homes happen to prevail in contemporary New Mexico. Oviedo claims, "These [northern New Mexico] people, they tell you they're traditional, but I don't know about [that] with their ways of life."

Oviedo's preference for traditional, that is, old-style, architecture has much more in common with elite Anglo taste than it does with the design choices of local community members. For Chimayósos who work at the "Lab" in Los Alamos, farm, or receive monthly government subsidies, the use of adobe is irrelevant to their everyday lives. It is hard work to make mud bricks, and the effort required to replaster houses nearly continuously is time consuming. To repair old houses is certainly more expensive than purchasing new aluminum ones, and it is more difficult to get a loan for an old house than for a trailer.

The adobe style of the Oviedos' house offers the same hand-hewn quality evident in the new addition to Centinela Traditional Arts. It is a quality other well-educated santeros know, too. In 1982, Félix López added an adobe workshop to his frame house in La Mesilla, complete with track lighting and sliding glass doors as well as old-style adobe *bancos* (benches) and *nichos* and a mud and straw floor. The application of contemporary amenities to new adobe constructions represents both a life-style and a degree of comfort that many local people can ill afford. The juxtaposition of modern conveniences and sleek design with old-style or genuinely old structures is an aesthetic and cultural preference of the twentieth-century Anglo elite,[20] a preference appropriated by urban or well-educated santeros.

Whether a monument to or a reinstatement of the past, the Oviedo

Fig. 84. Félix López in his studio, La Mesilla, 1992. Photo: Mary Peck.

Fig. 85. Trastero, 1992, by Ramón José López. Photo: Mary Peck.

CRAFTING DEVOTIONS

home is not entirely distanced from its locale. Before building the house, the Oviedos had to get its design approved by local officials. The Centinela settlement of Chimayó is part of Rio Arriba County, one of New Mexico's poorest. Historic building code restrictions do not apply there the way they do in Santa Fe. In Centinela, no museum professionals, state preservationists, or tourist agents participated in the approval process. Instead, local Chimayó officials considered the Oviedos' house design, assessing it with skepticism; few other two-story adobes exist in the county. Because, however, as Oviedo suggests, in Chimayó a reliance on fate and stoicism exists in place of building rules, the family was able to carry out their plan. Oviedo envisioned an image for the house, drew it on a paper bag, and presented it to the officials. The officials granted the Oviedos permission to build, in essence giving them the opportunity to create their own traditional style, one that may not have been accepted in a district more historically regulated.

Although they cater their business to a visiting clientele, the Oviedos also engage in the daily life of their village. Along with producing santos for sale to tourists, Marco makes handmade signs as gifts to local churches. Recently, the Oviedos also produced a reredos that they donated to a local church. When Marco and Patricia entertain visitors at Rancho de Chimayó Restaurant, they send their youngest son, J. J., down the hill to his grandmother's house, where he is fed homemade tacos and invited to spend the night. The Oviedos hang wool curtains woven by Jacobo Trujillo, who made blankets and rugs for tourist consumption, in the dining room of their home. Rather than serving as relics, art pieces, or souvenirs, the curtains in the Oviedos' house maintain utilitarian and familial value. When Oviedo's brother-in-law Irvin tells him, "Gosh, you can handle these [local] people," Marco responds, "I am these people. . . . Sharing is what life is all about. If you are like a merchant, it won't work."

PRODUCING SAINTS

Marco, his mother, Patricia, and their four children work as a team making images of saints. Marco, however, does most of the production. In the early 1980s, Oviedo initiated his family's santo-making enterprise, and today, he is the only family member who works at it full time. Patricia has a forty-hour-a-week job in Los Alamos, the children all go to school, and Marco's mother, Angélica López Oviedo, spends much of her time tending to household chores. Marco divides his time between managing Paseo de la Tierra Vieja and carving wood. He views his work with the animals and with the saints as an integrated, traditional way of life.

Like other contemporary santeros, such as Félix López, Charles Carrillo, Ramón José López, and Horacio Valdez, Oviedo prides himself on fashioning his santos according to the techniques and materials used by the Spanish colonial wood-carvers. Like the early-twentieth-century modernists, contemporary carvers attach a quality of authenticity to old or "primitive" pieces. They value replicas of original santos. Oviedo recognizes an inevitable distinction between the particular enhancements he adds to his contemporary replicas and actual historic pieces, yet he relies on the earlier wood-carvings as models.

Like the Spanish colonial santeros, Oviedo depends on the natural environment for resources with which to make santos. At least once a year, he makes "wood runs" to Borrego Mesa, in the peaks of the nearby Truchas Moun-

Fig. 86. Retablo in relief of San Geronimo (Saint Jerome), 1992, by Charles M. Carrillo, Ponderosa pine, natural pigments, piñon sap and grain alcohol varnish. Collection: JoAnn and Robert Balzer. Photo: Mary Peck.

tains, collecting cottonwood, aspen, and pine. If the wood is green, Oviedo lets it dry until it is ready for carving. Even after the wood dries sufficiently, however, Oviedo selects only about 20 percent of it for carving. Dried and cured are not enough; he wants the wood to be predictable. The wood-carver must be able to follow the grain of the woods to ensure that delicate protuberances, such as fingers, will not eventually break off.[21]

Oviedo uses power tools to cut down big logs and then uses hand tools, such as rasps, saws, axes, chisels, adzes, and Exacto knives, to carve his santos. He uses an electric drill to make holes for dowels. In earlier times, carvers used broken pieces of glass to smooth their works. Today, Oviedo, or more often his mother, smooths his pieces with sandpaper. If the figure is to be painted, as most of Oviedo's pieces are, the sanding is preparation for a first coat of hide glue. This is a combination of glue from rabbit hides, fish tails, and cowhides, mixed with water and then heated. Brushed on, it functions as a sizing element to provide more surface to which subsequent layers of gesso will adhere. It also seals the piece against humidity. Oviedo may apply as many as seven coats of glue on a carving, sanding between each coat. He coats the entire carving with this mixture, except for the bottom, which he leaves uncovered to allow the piece to "breathe" and avoid cracking. Once he coats the piece with the glue, Oviedo lets it dry for at least a week.

After the glue dries, Oviedo applies gesso, which becomes a base for the paint. Gesso not only makes the wood impervious to the water-soluble pigments the Oviedos use, but it can also correct small mistakes. Cans of gesso are readily available in hardware and art supply stores. But the Oviedos make their own, using rock gypsum they collect from an old mine south of Santa Fe. Like green wood, freshly mined gypsum is not immediately ready for use. It must be oven-baked to soften and become powder before the santero can use it. To make gesso, Oviedo mixes gypsum powder with animal glue. The amount and type of undercoats used on santos varies among santeros. Oviedo generally applies eight coats on each piece and then brushes a stabilizing solution of egg whites over that before he considers a carving ready for paint.[22]

The Oviedo children are learning to work in polychrome; however, Patricia Oviedo takes the major responsibility for skillfully painting the family santos. The husband and wife attribute Patricia's painting ability to her father Jacobo, whose talent for creating beautiful palettes was considered among his greatest strengths. Patricia makes paints primarily from natural pigments she collects locally. These include iron oxides, cadmium and mercury salts, walnut hull extract, and marigolds.[23] She also uses imported indigo and the cochineal bug. Usually, each carving takes three to four coats of pigment. Just as colonial santeros often varnished their pieces, the Oviedos finish their carvings with five coats of wax. Marco prefers beeswax and piñon sap. Other carvers, including Félix López, Charles Carrillo, and Victor Goler use a mixture of piñon sap and grain alcohol.

According to Patricia, her painting is a form of prayer. Marco says that "making saints is spiritual, sentimental, less technical." Other artists, particularly Zoraida Ortega of Velarde, consider painting santos a form of benediction. According to Mrs. Ortega, if one is not at peace with one's self, one cannot carve.[24]

Like Patricia Oviedo, Zoraida Ortega paints the santos her husband, Eulogio, carves. Within the past few years, both Oviedo and Ortega have begun to co-sign the santos they make with their husbands. Other women carvers, such

Fig. 87. Cristo, 1991, by Victor Goler, wood, paint, piñon sap and grain alcohol varnish. Collection: Gene Autry Western Heritage Museum. Photo: Susan Einstein.

< **Fig. 88.** Combined bulto and retablo of Nativity, 1991, by Eulogio and Zoraida Ortega. Like Marco and Patricia Oviedo, Eulogio and Zoradia Ortega work as a santo-making team. Eulogio carves images and Zoraida paints them. Zoraida Ortega also weaves Spanish colonial–style textiles. Collection: Gene Autry Western Heritage Museum. Photo: Susan Einstein

Fig. 89. Gloria López Córdova's workshop with santos in production, Córdova, 1991. Courtesy Gloria López Córdova. Photo: Mary Peck.

as Gloria López Córdova of Córdova, have also recently become recognized for their saint-making abilities. Córdova, who learned to carve from her famous uncle, George López, began her career by working anonymously for him. Today, she has her own carving establishment and signs her work independently of any family members. Her husband helps her, and her son makes his own wood carvings. Marie Romero Cash and her sister, Anita Romero Jones, among the first women santeras, have always had their own carving businesses. Their parents, Senaida and Emilio Romero, are well-known tin workers.

The Oviedo children help produce the family's santos. The oldest, Oliver, makes hand-hewn bases for the wood carvings. He also does all the ironwork and chips the obsidian needed for certain saints and other figures. The three younger children even produce images on their own. Daisy makes retablos. The two younger boys, Tony and J. J., carve their own bultos. Marco maintains a strong conviction that he must teach his skills to his children, the next generation. Yet at the same time that Oviedo de-emphasizes the commercial aspect of his santo production in favor of passing on a legacy, his children know that when they make santos for Spanish Market they have the potential to make extra spending money, an immediate and practical concern.

THE OVIEDO GALLERY

When the Oviedos built their house, they sold their carvings from the living room. On a table, they arranged a small display of the types of their carvings, along with the materials used to paint them, and a sequence of santos that demonstrated the process of carving from beginning to end. Although in this setting visitors did not get a glimpse of where the family actually works, and they were merely provided with a repetitive script that the carvers give to all visitors, they nonetheless received an introduction to the craft in the artists' private living quarters. No matter that serious carving did not take place there, and no matter that the presentation was made specifically for them. Eventually this mode of presentation got in the way of other family activities, so the Oviedos built the studio, which they also call the art gallery. The Oviedos required all tourists to enter the house through the gallery rather than in the living room, and in so doing, defied the false front that their living room conveyed. Whereas in the living room the santos appeared as if they were in a museum setting, in the gallery they actually are exhibited.

The gallery first opened to the public in 1990, built in what had been a two-car garage. To create the gallery, the family covered the interior walls of the garage with a combination of Moorish and New Mexican plaster, a mixture of mud and straw, built a floor of native Ponderosa pine boards, and made a ceiling of wood panels, vigas, and corbels. The Oviedos designed the gallery with many native details. They stained the floor with kerosene and placed a Chimayó rug over a section of it. In one section, they built a small portal, lowering the roof to enclose the space. The materials of this low ceiling consist of *latillas* (wood lath),

Fig. 90. Collectors' display of *Our Lady on a Cross,* n.d., by Marie Romero Cash, wood, paint, tin. Courtesy Bud and Barbara Hoover. Photo: Mary Peck.

Fig. 91. Daisy Oviedo with her retablo of the Holy Trinity, 1991 Spanish Market. Photo: Miguel A. Gandert.

Fig. 92. Marco Oviedo in his art gallery, with educational display about santo-making, Chimayó, 1991. The completed bulto at the end of the display is San Pascual (Saint Pascal), a devout shepherd who became a Franciscan laybrother and worked in the dining room and who Marco casually identifies as the patron saint of kitchens. San Pascual, smiling and holding a skillet, is among the Oviedos' most popular santos. In the three *nichos* above San Pascual are two images, to the left and right, of San Santiago (Saint James the Greater) and, in the middle, a bulto of La Divina Pastora (The Good Shepherdess). Photo: Mary Peck.

CRAFTING DEVOTIONS

although they are more decorative than functional. The house's second story lies above the gallery, and therefore the *latillas* do not support a mud roof. Instead, they hide plumbing pipes for the house.

For displaying santos, Oviedo and his children incorporated *nichos* in the gallery walls. One section, intended to replicate a chapel, has a slightly raised floor with a railing in front of it and *nichos* on the wall. Oviedo hired two friends, Rick and Susan Bell, to design the gallery lighting. This couple, who Oviedo met when they happened to stop at his house to look at wood carvings, are professional museum exhibition designers.

The Oviedo gallery is beautiful. It is pristine and has the "native look" so valued by patrons of the Santa Fe style. According to Oviedo, the windows are part of the whole effect. One could even regard them as the equivalent of picture windows in a bus, with the art gallery itself representing a luxury vehicle. Oviedo claims that New Yorkers are especially taken with the panoramic view the windows provide of the Chimayó landscape.

Two blue banners flank the door to the Oviedo art gallery, identifying it as the studio entrance. Another door next to the gallery serves as the entry into the Oviedo house. Each door has a bell; however, the bell for the home is mechanized, whereas the one for the studio is a dinner bell that lets the family know, wherever they are on the property, when a visitor approaches.

Marco's mother often answers when the doorbells ring. If tourists come to the door that leads into the house, Angélica Oviedo, or whoever else answers, directs them to the studio entrance. The tourists' questions allow Mrs. Oviedo to determine the visitors' familiarity with carving and ascertain their potential as customers. If she thinks they want to make a purchase, she calls her son to greet them. Marco then explains the range of the family's repertoire and the authenticity of his carvings, showing likenesses between his works and those displayed in exhibition catalogues and other museum publications. For Oviedo, replication of older pieces suggests legitimacy in new ones. He has displayed two replicas—La Muerte in a *nicho* and a bulto of San Acacio—that are both featured in George Mills's book *The People of the Saints* and are part of the permanent collection of the Taylor Museum.[25] Oviedo's comment about his muerte is, "This is a fantastic piece. This is a new piece, but it looks old."

Oviedo discusses more than his replicas, however. He has an entire discourse reserved for visitors, calling his presentation "like a school for some people." He tells them, "We do five things." In other words, the Oviedos produce five types of carvings. After Marco shows replicas, his first category of carving, he then describes his "folkloric pieces." These pieces are not necessarily historic saints, he explains. Rather, they are "in the area." They are Marco's and other local people's interpretations of santos and narratives from the region. Marco carves his folkloric pieces in his own style, decorating them with native materials, such as mica or obsidian. He cites his San Pascual as an example. Oviedo says this santo existed "historically," but "now he is in the public domain." San Pascual was a Third Order Franciscan who occasionally worked in the monastery kitchen. Devoted more to the Eucharist and Christ than he was to food preparation, San Pascual is nevertheless remembered today as the patron saint of cooking. Oviedo carves him holding a skillet and markets him as a "saint you can put in your kitchen," considering this santo a more mundane collectible than, say, a collectors' item.[26]

Another example of a folkloric piece is Oviedo's Madona de Santa Fe.

Overleaf

Left

Fig. 93. Interior, Oviedo art gallery, Chimayó, 1991. The design of this gallery reflects a combination of ideas about presenting and selling local Hispano tradition. On the wooden lintel above the window, Oviedo engraved a figure copied from ancient Mimbres Indian pottery. Below this engraving sits a bronze cast Marco made of the same Mimbres figure. On the right is an altarlike setting, complete with Spanish colonial–style church railings and a *nicho* for placing santos. The white pedestal that supports the Carretta de la Muerte emphasizes the museumized quality of the setting. On the wall adjacent to the railing is a framed copy of a local newspaper article about the historical significance Patricia attaches to her burro rides. Courtesy Marco and Patricia Oviedo. Photo: Mary Peck.

Right

Fig. 94. *La Muerte* (Death figure), ca. 1980s, by Marco Oviedo. Courtesy Marco and Patricia Oviedo. Marco prides himself on the likeness between his image of La Muerte and its nineteenth-century prototype in the Taylor Museum exhibition catalogue, *The People of the Saints*. Photo: Mary Peck.

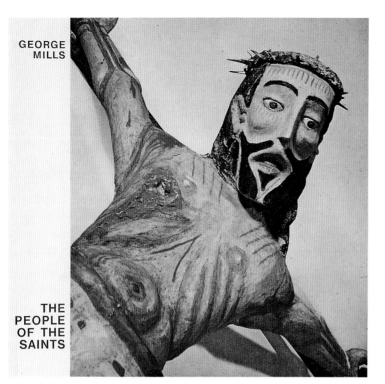

GEORGE
MILLS

THE
PEOPLE
OF THE
SAINTS

Fig. 95. Book cover for *People of the Saints,* by
George Mills, and plate 12, *La Muerte,* in *People
of the Saints.* Collection: Gene Autry Western
Heritage Museum. Gift of Marco and Patricia
Oviedo. Photo: Mary Peck.

He fashions this after images of Santa Rita de Cascia and San Antonio made by the nineteenth-century carver the Santo Niño Santero. But the Madona also holds what Oviedo identifies as a Navajo squash blossom patterned from a flowering staff held by a bulto of San José by the master colonial santero, José Raphael Aragón.[27] She also carries a child dressed in turquoise. Oviedo refers to the squash blossom and the turquoise of the dress as "classic Indian attributes," and he considers them his "own inventions," inspired by the historic iconography of the piece. According to Oviedo, "After you've been carving a while, you can make up a few new figures."

Oviedo claims that "in the last couple of years, carvers have been doing different things." Inventing itself, as well as the new forms, is now part of New Mexico tradition. Oviedo points out Albuquerque santero Max Roybal as a carver who has produced images of soldiers as well as saints. Luis Tapia's figures of Hispano performers provide other examples.

Although at first glance one could deride producers of such "secular santos" for selling out, for accommodating their artistry to more commercial needs and to consumer preferences, on second glance, the production of "secular santos" broadens the producers' opportunities. Not all consumers of santos are devout Catholics. Because the twentieth-century market is as much a part of tradition as the santos themselves, the santeros must compete commercially for their production of images to survive. If they do not, their art will be left to the ethnic labeling, or stereotyping, of tourists and other "others." Contemporary wood-carvers' inventions may reflect an accommodation to the needs of a tourist clientele, but they also represent a minority taking control of its own identity.

The "really religious pieces" are the third category. Oviedo claims he puts less blood on his images of Christ than those produced in the Spanish colonial era, but he argues that "they're (still) really religious." According to Oviedo, the bloody pieces scare some people.

"Storytellers" is Oviedo's fourth category. These carvings "are not religious, but they depict activities in the old ways." Examples include *The Conquistadores*—images of pilgrims rather than soldiers—*Noah's Ark*, pieces he calls Penitente processions, and various groupings of old men, young boys, donkeys hauling wood, and dogs. Narrative rather than sacramental, storytellers as art forms have never functioned in a religious setting. The "beauty of the storytellers," claims Oviedo, is that "some people don't want religious images in their house." The storyteller line allows consumers to acquire New Mexican Hispano wood carvings without buying the religion that goes with them.

Oviedo's "bronzes" are his final category of wood carvings. Indeed, he does not make these santos of wood at all. They are cast-bronze statues made from wax molds that are themselves made from wood molds he carves. Until recently, Weston Foundry of Santa Fe produced the bronzes. Today, the family is creating their own foundry on their farm. Oviedo began producing bronzes in 1989 as a way to be more creative in his wood carving. The bronze production process allows him to put more detail into one carving and divide the cost among thirty-five pieces. It is more economical to carve one mold for casting limited editions than to reproduce identical santos in wood. Also, individual bronzes cost more than wood carvings. Further, Oviedo can produce a bronze in three to four weeks. A good wood polychrome, on the other hand, can take as many as twenty-four weeks, a week for each coat of paint.

Oviedo does not think he compromises the traditional appearance of

La Madona de Santa Fé
por
MARCO A. OVIEDO

santos when he changes the medium to bronze. The bronzes look like wood carvings thanks to the knife cuts in the casting molds and the patinas he claims to have "super researched" to achieve the same colors that his wooden santos have. Oviedo suggests that bronzes are more durable than wood, and this is why he produces them—for posterity. Besides, Oviedo anticipates that bronze artworks might appeal to an even larger Western-art buying public. Collectors of Native American and cowboy art, for example, purchase bronzes all the time. To best accommodate these patrons, Oviedo creates images other than saints. He has produced a bronze cast of a rain serpent image, copied from prehistoric Mimbres pottery designs rather than from a Spanish colonial source. For Oviedo, bronze sculpting of Native American and Hispano subjects is a way of keeping santo making alive in the late twentieth century.

With his bronzes, Oviedo also expands his own recognition and appreciation of art. In the Oviedos' living room are two bronze sculptures by Star Liana York. One is an image of a cowgirl on a horse, titled *Purina Princess.* The other is of a bison. Like Oviedo once did, York has her sculptures cast at Weston's foundry. Oviedo acquired York's bronzes by trading two of his works for hers.

The Oviedos collect paintings and bronzes. Like Luis Tapia and other contemporary carvers such as José Benjamín López, the Oviedos' santo production brings them into direct contact with the mainstream art world. Their acquisition of works such as York's signifies membership and participation in an elite culture.

When I asked Oviedo whether his wood carving represented a tradition or a profession, he replied,

> It's a traditional profession.... I put all my soul in the piece.... You can saturate [the] market. Any artist that has artistic ability, he has a tremendous responsibility to be honest. You can commercialize your own production. You can get so hungry.... Many people get so busy with orders that they can burn themselves [out]. The whole process of production needs to be well programmed. In my profession, I carve six—eight hours a day. You got to be responsible to "the business." If you get ill in forty or fifty years and you need to sell your Oviedo carving, it's got to be the best it can be.... It's a whole profession.

The Oviedos embrace the interest tourists find in their works, and they develop long-term relationships with people who come back and visit them over time. These visitors are generally serious collectors of the Oviedos' works and quite knowledgeable about Southwestern art. Most are Anglos. Some live in Santa Fe. Others come from all over the United States, making periodic visits to New Mexico, buying art. Although these relationships are indisputably unequal, in that the collectors have more money and power than the Oviedos, they are not necessarily temporary or superficial, two qualities that Dean MacCannell assigns to associations between tourists and local people.[28]

The Oviedos follow financial strategies of the elite gallery world. This includes taking advice from collectors, particularly from Robert Vogele of Chicago. Vogele was the first patron to visit the Oviedos in their new home. Having seen their work in private collections and museums, he immediately asked Oviedo to make a Noah's Ark like one owned by the Albuquerque Museum. Producing a Noah's Ark requires intensive labor. All the animals are made of exotic hardwoods and command a lot of detail carving. Oviedo obliged Vogele, and the two became friends. From Vogele's special interest in the Oviedos' work, the questions he asked about the family's means of production, and his seasoned experi-

Fig. 96. Bulto of Madona de Santa Fe, 1992, by Marco Oviedo, bronze cast from wax mold, patinas. Collection: Gene Autry Western Heritage Museum. Photo: Susan Einstein.

ence as a collector, Oviedo quickly learned that his new Chicago friend was a keen businessman. Oviedo asked Vogele to help him set up the business that would become his gallery. Vogele agreed, and the two devised a highly sophisticated method for pricing santos.

Essentially, Oviedo and Vogele established two price categories for the carvings. One is called a "studio price," designed for placing commissions. Carvings in this category usually take between four and six months to complete. "When someone places a commission, we give a 'studio price'; it's a low price." Oviedo asks for a deposit. "If I don't know the person—40 percent down. If it's easy to sell—twenty dollars down." On the other hand, "when someone is in a hurry, like for a gift, they pay a 'gallery price.' It's a little more expensive because they don't have to wait. That functions well." Oviedo charges a gallery price for a piece already completed. Gallery prices are at least 40 percent higher than studio prices.

In its elegance and beauty, the Oviedo art gallery is not unlike a new car showroom. Throughout the *nichos,* the Oviedos have their complete "line" of santos, other wood carvings, and bronzes on display. They literally walk their visitors around, showing examples of their five types of carvings. Just like new car buyers, visitors are sometimes offered special rates. These could be winter rates or off-season rates and are above and beyond the discount of the studio price. The Oviedos accept credit cards, and they do most of their business by taking orders. They have been so successful with sales that little in their showroom is actually for sale. Most is on loan to the carvers from patrons who have already purchased the works.

According to Oviedo, "When people come to Santa Fe, they have trouble finding quality. . . . The thing I try to do is put a little class. People think Hispanics are just lowriders." The Oviedos, who themselves have had the advantages of higher education and travel, use these experiences to gain the authority necessary to sell tradition. When I asked Oviedo, "What's your biggest seller?" he replied,

> It goes in seasons. San Pascual is really popular. [So are] the Death Cart and San Rafael. Storytellers are really popular. Some people feel uncomfortable around saints. Jewish people don't like Christian art at all. I don't think it's a matter of religion; it's a personal position. For a business like mine that has a bunch of Christian images, it's kind of touchy. They need to look at it as art. I'm not carving for religion, but for tradition. If [Jewish people] bring me a picture [of Moses], I'd be glad to do it. If patrons find something in a museum they want, I will try and replicate it.

As they befriend a variety of participants in the fine-art world, the Oviedos construct a past that meets contemporary expectations, including their own.

In his home, Marco Oviedo has mastered more than the art of making santos. He has mastered the art of living close to the land and being able to raise a family in late-twentieth-century northern New Mexico. He may have followed the expectations of tourists in creating his business, but he has also relied on his own independence and creativity. Art galleries such as his may not have existed in the Spanish colonial era, but they are as much an ethnographic fact in the late twentieth century as historic-style homes and burro rides. In the Oviedo art gallery, tradition itself, not just the Spanish colonial heritage, is put on display. As such, the gallery encapsulates general Chimayó cultural production.

As he takes me through his gallery and turns on the sound system in a closet attached to the art space, Oviedo explains that he tries to provide atmo-

Fig. 97. *Penitente Procession,* 1988, by Marco and Patricia Oviedo. Blue ribbon for first prize, 1988 Spanish Market. Marco classifies this carving, which depicts a Holy Week procession by members of the Brotherhood of Our Father Jesus, as a storyteller, because of its narrative rather than sacramental quality. Photo: Richard D. Wickstrom.

sphere for people, "from the visual to [the] listening to what I tell people." He likens a visit to his house to a packaged tour. When visitors come, the Oviedos do not only show wood carvings. They offer a total experience. For example, "In apple time, [visitors] go and pick apples with us. They take donkey rides; they go to Rancho de Chimayó to eat with us. That's the package, the whole thing."

Most of the people who come to the Oviedos' are patrons, school groups, and general tourists. But increasingly, formal tour groups also schedule trips to the Oviedo home. Organizations such as Crow Canyon Tours, Rojo Tours, and Discover Santa Fe visit. Oviedo prefers these scheduled visits, because they give him more control over the way he plans his day. And he likes the particular companies who come. Crow Canyon Tours, run by a professional archaeologist from Colorado, "bring people who really have the interest. . . . Rojo Tours brings people here—sometimes just one person—they really want to see you. . . . You feel good if you have a chance to talk [with these people]." He further clarifies, "I don't receive buses yet. The Crow Canyons . . . this is really exclusive."

As he distinguishes the touring companies from bus tours, Oviedo betrays a qualitative evaluation based at least partially on the tourists' social class. In spite of Oviedo's selective stance, however, he remains a tour guide. Participants in Rojo Tours, Crow Canyon Tours, and Discover Santa Fe may, like ethnographers, be educated and in search of "true experience," but they are nonetheless participants in what Daniel Boorstin has called a "psuedo-event," an "elaborately contrived indirect experience, an artificial product to be consumed in the very places where the real thing is as free as air."[29] Still, as the Oviedos respond to serious questions from curious visitors whom they consider interesting, they work within the confines and structure of tourism to achieve some sort of interpersonal solidarity between themselves and their visitors.[30]

Not only have touring companies discovered the Oviedo farm, but the establishment is significantly mapped out in the annual *Collector's Guide to Santa Fe & Taos*.[31] The Oviedos have a full-color half-page advertisement in the guide, identifying them as "Oviedo Carvings and Bronze. Marco Oviedo and Family. A family of carvers since 1730." A photograph shows the range of the family's wood carvings, including a Penitente "storyteller" with a blue ribbon lying on it, which Oviedo won at the 1988 Spanish Market. Directions, hours of operation, an address, and phone number complete the information. The ad is numbered and keyed to one of the many tourist maps provided in the guide. Oviedo Carvings and Bronze and Santos of New Mexico by Charles M. Carrillo are the only contemporary wood carving studios that are part of the official art cartography of northern New Mexico.[32]

Advertised in the Santa Fe *Collector's Guide*, the Oviedo and Carrillo studios are keyed into the larger literature on mainstream art. Carrillo's ad describes him as an "award-winning santero" who produces "museum-quality santos made with home-made pigments, cottonwood root and hand-adzed panels." He is listed as an exhibitor at Spanish Market each year and in the permanent collections of four major national museums. The ad, which integrates museums, awards, and handmade art, reflects the interests of late-twentieth-century ethnography and tourism. The select appearance of the Carrillo and Oviedo studios in the *Collectors' Guide* isolates them from their surrounding environs and treats them as being analogous to museums and galleries.

SANTOS OF NEW MEXICO
BY
CHARLES M. CARRILLO
AWARD-WINNING SANTERO

Museum-quality traditional New Mexican santos made with home-made pigments, cottonwood root and hand-adzed panels

EXHIBITOR AT SPANISH MARKET
Santa Fe Plaza each year during the last full weekend of July

IN PERMANENT COLLECTIONS
Museum of American History · Smithsonian
Museum of International Folk Art · Santa Fe
Millicent Rogers Museum · Taos
Gene Autry Western Heritage Museum · LA
The Heard Museum · Phoenix

STUDIO BY APPOINTMENT
2712 PASEO DE TULAROSA
SANTA FE, NEW MEXICO 87505
505·473·7941

Photo: Ron Behrmann

"Altar de Penitencia"   7' x 4'
Ponderosa pine, natural pigments, piñon sap varnish

Fig. 98. Advertisement for Santos of New Mexico by Charles M. Carrillo, in *1991-1992 Collector's Guide to Santa Fe & Taos*. Altar de Penitencia (Altar of Penance), ca. 1991, by Charles M. Carrillo. Photo of altar: Ron Behrmann. Courtesy Charles M. Carrillo and Wingspread Communications. Photo of advertisement: James Hart.

On first reading, the Oviedos' business provides entertainment, edification, and sales. It is nonoppositional and even suggests an acceptance of hegemonic control over the Spanish colonial image. However, underlying this is another, slightly more oppositional, message. The funny signs, Patricia's jokes, and even the rhetoric in their gallery betray the Oviedos' sophistication at creating an attractive display for tourists, but they also reveal the family's effective critique of their trade and of their visitors and their strategies for protecting their privacy while selling to visitors.[33]

Just as tourists and ethnographers come to the Oviedos with an interest in taking some part of the site back to their own cultural milieu, either in the form of a wood carving, field notes, or a general "authentic experience," the Oviedos provide their own version of presentations they anticipate visitors to expect. By parodying directional signs, explorations of ancient sites, and even holy religious images (i.e., such as the image of San Pascual, a "saint you can put in your kitchen"), the Oviedos exaggerate the follies of their "other." By switching the content in their directional signs from children, deer, and zoo animals to donkeys and mules, the Oviedos, as tricksters, offer an effective rebuttal to their visitors, begging the question, Who is the ass, the animal as subject or the visitor? And who really is the observed? The tourist or the Oviedos and their donkeys?

The Oviedos' tricksterism serves two functions. First, their burlesque of their visitors strengthens their own sense of cultural identity. It allows them to laugh at what they hope they are not.[34] Although they rely on the marketing strategies of the elite art world, the Oviedos do not necessarily embrace the dominant culture. Second, by using the predictable expectations of tourists as their starting point of communication, the Oviedos can sometimes cajole their visitors into seeing them as human beings just like the tourists. On the other hand, the joke about the cow-dinosaurs, the symbolic inversion apparent in the directional signs, and even the marketing categories of the santos for sale represent levels of meaning that are not necessarily intended for the casual visitor. Rather, they are essentially for the Oviedos or others "in the know."[35]

The Oviedo family of carvers has become very successful over the last ten years as producers of Spanish colonial–style saints and as performers of rural village life. In the words of a Chimayó neighbor who also deals in santos and tourism, Marco is "class itself. He has a very good sense of how to do things." A comment Marco makes about one of the outbuildings on his place, a barnlike structure used for storage, carpentry, welding, and, most recently, casting points to his attitudes regarding self-sufficiency and creativity. Oviedo says of his barn, "A little ranch like [ours] needs to have a hell of a shop. We do all the construction."

Indeed, Marco Oviedo does all the construction on his farm, but this entails far more than building a house, burro stalls, and wood carvings. With the help of his family, Oviedo constructs a reality. The family's replicas of religious art, housing, farming, and a gallery may represent an ideal of tradition, but it is their copying that creates the origin.[36] The Oviedos may promise the presence of authenticity, but all they can deliver is their invention and representation.

Because, as Kirshenblatt-Gimblett argues, real life is elusive in the face of tourism, the success of the Oviedos' site lies not in how real the attractions are, but in how authoritative the production has become.[37] The Chimayó neighbor and dealer who praises Oviedo offers one explanation of the craftsman's success:

At the same time that his carvings are naïve and primitive, they're very slick. [The] bronze color—is a nice antique color. [Although] it's taking the sincerity and moving it one step further, and that's the problem with religious folk art,...I like what Oviedo's doing. I like the way he's keeping the tradition alive. From an outsider's point of view, they're real attractive, but for me, they're real slick. I applaud him for his insight.... [He] shows just enough of the chip carving but also shows [the santos] as lifelike as possible.... If you move to another country, you bring your own individual reference points and approach the tradition with objectivity. A doctor [Marco] coming into a rural community, he has potential unlike many of his neighbors. [He has the] ability to have some contrast.

The authoritative power of the Oviedos' representation of their past and present is undeniable. Their home site is economically and socially viable. The family's invocations of a supposed prior reality, including Patricia's descent from Spanish colonial settlers and Marco's wood-carving forebears, represent historical narratives transformed into a personal narrative that the Oviedos, through a lot of hard work, have gained the right to tell.[38]

Like the different categories and prices of santos the family sells, the front and back regions at the Oviedos are negotiable, depending on the nature of the relationships the Oviedos and their visitors form. The Oviedos, who have defined and marked the spaces where their visitors are permitted to go, have the option of offering people a more intimate glimpse of their lives. For example, all tourists who have not yet met the Oviedos are immediately directed to the studio entrance, the formal space that some tourists attempt to get behind. Tourists who have become friends with the Oviedos may be invited to pass completely beyond the studio entrance and call on the Oviedos at the living room door. Very close friends of the Oviedos or trusted field workers might even have access to the interior of the barn, a back region that could offer insight into the everyday activities of the family in an ethnographic sense.

Within the context of tourism, the Oviedos structure the kinds of relationships they wish to have. A popular image of Spanish colonial life is theirs alone, either to repeat in a mechanical way or to reveal as touristic rhetoric to visitors who come to see them. This choice gives them power. The Oviedos arrange their farm according to the demands of a tourist trade, but their reflexive awareness of their situation offers them not only privacy from visitors but also a chance for their own self-definition.

4

Enrique Rendón:
A Folk Artist's
Folk Artist

Enrique Rendón (1923–87) of Velarde began carving images of saints out of wood in the 1970s. Retired at age fifty-one and reliant on a disability pension, Rendón supplemented his income by producing santos and selling them to various patrons. Images of saints played a key role in his spiritual life. Enrique Rendón was a devout Catholic, and for the last eight years of his life, he served as the *hermano mayor* (elder brother), or superior in charge, of the nearby Lyden morada, the meetinghouse of the local chapter of the Brotherhood of Our Father Jesus.

Like many contemporary carvers, Enrique Rendón made religious images to sell. He viewed his santos as commercial products that involved economic transactions. Unlike most santeros concerned with sales, however, Rendón did not participate in public markets and crafts fairs. Neither the individual style nor the form of Rendón's santos corresponded to the self-conscious revival of Spanish colonial art required of Spanish Market and other crafts-fair participants: he compromised neither his own creativity nor his particular marketing techniques for the approval of an outside panel of market judges. Instead, Rendón sold most of his work from his home. He displayed many of his carvings on a metal cart in his living room and welcomed visitors in to see his crafts. Although selling from one's home was not novel—indeed, the early revival artists began by presenting their work this way in the 1920s and many contemporary carvers, like the Oviedos and Luisito Luján, continue the practice today—Rendón's style of doing so, with disregard for the Anglo patrons and promoters who controlled the public markets, was novel. Rendón eventually began to show and sell his work at El Potrero Trading Post in nearby Chimayó, but the proprietors of the

Fig. 99. Enrique Rendón, Velarde, 1983. Photo: Laurie Beth Kalb.

OPPOSITE

Fig. 100. Display of Luisito Luján's carvings, Nambé, 1992. When visitors arrive at Luján's home, which is where he grew up, the artist immediately brings them to the room where he displays his santos, inviting them to sign his guest book and generally making them feel welcome. Separate from his commissions, the carvings on the table are completed according to Luján's prerogative. Some have been on view for years; others are recent additions. In spite of Luján's strong attachments to some of these images, most are for sale. Luján's public presentation of his santos at his home recalls Enrique Rendón's presentational style in Velarde. Photo: Mary Peck.

store were not outsiders. They were members of a local Hispano family who until recently had little communication with the elite Santa Fe art community.

Enrique Rendón became a model of authenticity for other contemporary santeros and friends. To Rendón's local acquaintances, authenticity had more to do with spontaneity and love than with reproduction and replication of past styles and adherence to an original ideal. Carvers such as his neighbor Eulogio Ortega point to Rendón's images as the only ones that "came directly from the spirit and [were] not a copy of anything." Velarde santo collector Raymond Smith claims, "I loved Henry's work because it reminded me of two hundred years ago. . . . It was a labor of love."

Rendón remained one step removed from the self-conscious revival of other twentieth-century santeros. Rather than search for authenticity in his craft, he created his own. He drew on his individual experiences, including religion, personal acquaintances, and other passions such as travel, for inspiration in his work. Rendón also participated with tradition by appropriating elements of popular culture and inheriting expressions of the past. He relied on mass-produced objects, such as plastic ornaments and manufactured knick-knacks, as well as natural materials, such as cottonwood and aspen, for creating his saints. He marketed his images while paying close attention to proper iconography. This complexity, this tangle of the market and the spiritual, enabled Rendón to continue production of a type of object that is now commodified yet nonetheless a vital part of his own group's history.[1]

This chapter demonstrates how mass production, consumerism, religion, *and* aesthetics were all deeply embedded in Enrique Rendón's santos. I show how he refused to depend on an outside market for his craft, yet how Anglo commercial values were a part of his own tradition. Enrique Rendón's craft represented a cultural current that ran obliquely to, not oppositionally against, the packaging of heritage so prevalent in contemporary northern New Mexico. His santos were concurrently commercial, aesthetic, religious, self-parodying, and, ultimately, irreducible to one or even a few descriptive categories. They were out of keeping with the smooth surfaces of authenticity attempted by other, more officially recognized, santeros.[2]

BEGINNINGS

Enrique Rendón was born on 2 October 1923 in Monero, New Mexico. Monero is a coal mining community located less than ten miles south of the Colorado line and a good three hours drive northwest from the fruit-raising village of Velarde, where Rendón lived continuously for more than twenty years until his death in 1987. Velarde is situated along Highway 64 between the two northern New Mexico urban centers of Española and Taos. The village of Velarde is not heavily visited by tourists; however, local Hispano farmers raise apples, peaches, and other fruit there as market crops, and fruit stands dot the highway, allowing farmers to sell uneven yields to tourists and other travelers.[3]

Although Rendón is an old Hispano New Mexican name, the place name *Monero*, Rendón's home town, is an Italian word for money. When the town

Fig. 101. Eulogio Ortega in front of his wood-carving shop, Velarde, 1992. The carver sits under one of the many apple trees that comprise his fruit orchard in the fertile Rio Grande river valley of Velarde. Photo: Mary Peck.

was settled in 1884, a number of Italians lived there.[4] In the late nineteenth century, not only Anglo-Americans from the Northeast arrived in New Mexico, but also European immigrants—particularly Germans, Italians, and French—traveled west for money via the American South. Since this time of settlement, many Europeans have acculturated themselves into local Hispano life and acquired the use of New Mexican Spanish.

The Rendón family moved permanently to Velarde in the mid-1940s. Before settling in the Rio Grande village, they spent summers there with members of Enrique's mother's family. Miguel Rendón (1859–1929), Enrique's father, worked for the Denver and Rio Grande Railroad, which had tracks running through the northwestern part of the state. He and his wife Celsa Valdez (Rendón) Herrera (1898–1990) had four children. After Miguel died, Celsa married Gorgonio Herrera and had one daughter. Enrique's two sisters, Cordelia and Esther, and his half-sister, Dulcinea, live in Velarde today. Their brother Leo lives in Utah. Two of Rendón's sisters have maintained active roles in Velarde. Until recently, Cordelia owned and operated the local café called the Apple Valley Bar. Dulcinea knows many people in the area through the mobile-home lots she and her husband Joe López rent out and through her participation in local recreational activities, including bowling and bingo.

Enrique Rendón was educated in New Mexico. At the age of seventeen, he started work in coal mines there and in Utah and Colorado. He also worked in Los Alamos, New Mexico, and for the Union Pacific Railroad. From 1962 until his retirement in 1974, Rendón worked as a custodian in the Velarde public elementary school.[5] Zoraida Ortega also worked at the elementary school as a teacher.

Fig. 102. Dulcinea López and Margaret Gutierrez, Velarde, 1991. Photo: Mary Peck.

She remembers Rendón fondly as a friend and as a good worker. According to Eulogio Ortega, Rendón especially liked Zoraida. He "always made her classroom shine."[6]

Rendón never explained what it was that made him carve, and he resisted a romantic image of his artistic motives. Nevertheless, Ortega suggests that it was a "creative energy within [Rendón] that gradually came out." Ortega says that Rendón began his artwork by making little men and animals from burrs he collected in the fields and then stuck together. After that, he made miniature furniture out of tin or aluminum. He used beer cans or any type of tin he could find and "very cleverly cut it with scissors and [made] a chair or a bed out of one piece of tin. . . . Some of the tiny dressers even had a mirror glued on."

Ortega believes Rendón began making santos after seeing images by Horacio Valdez, who also began carving santos in the mid-1970s, after a nearly fatal accident badly crushed his right hand and caused him to give up carpentry.[7] Valdez was a faithful member of the Lyden morada for a time. In the mid-1970s, when Rendón and Valdez were active in the brotherhood, they were very good friends. During this time, Ortega recalls occasionally meeting the two men in Española, eating together in a restaurant.[8]

Eulogio Ortega claims that Rendón was prolific in his saint making. He began carving and painting santos before he ever thought of selling them. Ortega remembers that Rendón "had so many santos at one time, before he began to sell them. We [Eulogio and Zoraida] used to like to go to his house and see them all over the house with those piercing eyes that [were] his trademark."[9]

For the last twenty years of his life, Rendón lived in a five-room, L-shaped adobe house with nineteen-inch-thick walls and doors leading outside from every room except the corner kitchen. More than a mere representation, Rendón's home *was* a house from the late nineteenth or early twentieth century.[10] Joe López, Rendón's brother-in-law, dates the house to at least the turn of the century. Rendón acquired the house from his second wife, Sara Martínez, who obtained it from her mother. Until Rendón's death, succeeding generations of the Martínez family continuously occupied the house.

Rendón's house had significance for his family and friends because of its Spanish colonial design and pattern of use based on family inheritance and lineage. The dwelling and the historical moment it represented formed a sort of unity for Rendón, marked by his ongoing personal connections to it. It was a part of the past entirely continuous with the wood-carver's contemporary social experience. For other santeros, Rendón's house signified a folk form and a notion of tradition that they strove to recreate.[11] One enthusiast even wanted to buy the house from Rendón.

RENDÓN AND THE CARVING INDUSTRY

Rendón began carving santos toward the end of his tenure at the Velarde public school. Most contemporary carvers either gather together to share wood-carving ideas or participate in markets and network with collectors, but Rendón's

Fig. 103. Enrique Rendón's five-room, L-shaped adobe house, Velarde, ca. 1900. Photo: Laurie Beth Kalb, ca. 1986.

Fig. 104. Display of santos by Horacio Valdez in Raymond and Viola Smith's home, Velarde, 1992. Bultos (left to right) of San Rafael Arcángel (Saint Raphael Archangel), 1985, and Our Lady Queen of the Skies, 1984. Courtesy Raymond and Viola Smith. Photo: Mary Peck.

carving was a solitary pursuit. He had neither a professional background such as carpentry, like Horacio Valdez, nor family ties to a wood-carving tradition that would explain his production of saints. He did not advertise his activities, nor did he rely on his santo making for a link to his ethnic identity. Rendón made images of saints because he loved them and because he liked to carve. In his retirement, Rendón claimed that the production of saints "help[ed] . . . to keep [my] mind busy," and he could regulate his work at his own slow, but regular, pace.

Unlike the Oviedos and other Chimayó craftspeople who advertise their trades and define their histories with numerous site markers, no signs directed visitors to Rendón's house. In fact, with the exception of the Ortegas' house, no markers accommodating tourists exist at all in Velarde. Eulogio Ortega guided my first visit to Rendón's home by driving me there. Other friends and patrons learned where Rendón lived in a similar, informal way. Raymond Smith heard about Rendón's carvings through word of mouth. Horacio Valdez, whose work Smith also collected, described Rendón's work and told Smith where the santero lived.

Although he kept to himself as a santero, Enrique Rendón was held in high esteem by other contemporary carvers. Santeros praised him for his individual style and independent spirit, recommending him to researchers and collectors. Two important early exhibitions of contemporary Hispano art, especially the 1983 Galeria de la Raza exhibit, "Santos de New Mexico," included his work. This show emphasized issues of artistic freedom espoused by the young Chicano artists who formed La Escuela Artesana.

One of the most significant manifestations of Rendón's independent spirit was his avoidance of Anglo-dominated art markets. Although he exhibited

Fig. 105. Santos by Enrique Rendón, displayed in Potrero Trading Post, Chimayó, 1991. Three images on the bottom shelf depict San Calletano (Saint Cajetan), cofounder of the Theatine Order and patron of gamblers. One image is painted, another is varnished, and a third is left unpainted. On the unpainted santo, incising, or chip-carving, replaces paint as a decorative device. Although he loved to embellish his carvings with color and miniature objects, Rendón left some of his work unpainted at the request of Elma Bal, the proprietor of Potrero Trading Post, who occasionally commissioned him. Potrero Trading Post serves many customers, including devout Catholics and recreational travelers who have little interest in religion. Mrs. Bal requested unpainted santos to meet tourist demands. The Bal collection of Rendón's santos has not been available for sale since the woodcarver's death. On the wall above Rendón's saints hangs an unpainted carving by a Córdova artist. At the far right is part of a retablo with a tin frame by Anita Romero Jones. Below the retablo and behind Rendón's santos are bead necklaces imported from Africa. Collection: Raymond Bal. Photo: Mary Peck.

in art galleries and museums, Rendón never participated in the Spanish Market and he entered the Albuquerque Feria Artesana only once. According to Eulogio Ortega, Rendón never even went to the Santa Fe Spanish Market as a visitor. Rendón recognized that his style was different, that it conformed to neither the unpainted and iconographically meager images initiated in the 1920s nor to the current replicas of nineteenth-century church icons; however, he was not affected by the design choices of other carvers. He found pleasure in his unusual style and enjoyed the appreciation others had of it. Besides, Rendón felt that he had no need to sell at these fairs. In contrast to the lofty notion that patrons and some carvers had of the art fairs as social gathering places for artists, Rendón viewed the fairs as pure sellers' markets. Within this commercial context, Rendón suggested that the fairs were a waste of time. On one occasion, he complained about the organization of the Feria Artesana, where patrons could not collect their purchases until the end of the weekend so the works could be kept on display. According to Rendón, this rule discouraged sales.

If Rendón noticed contradictions in the commercial venues for selling santos, Eulogio Ortega suggested that Rendón also encountered what he considered disparities in the more radical, grass-roots carving organizations. Rendón never participated in La Cofradía de Artes y Artesanos Hispanicos, but he attended a few meetings of the Española Escuelita, which he was invited to join. However, a particular incident that occurred at one of his first Escuelita sessions insulted Rendón so that he rejected the group and never went back. Ortega remembers laughing when Rendón told him that one of the Escuelita members, a wood-carver not inclined toward carving santos, produced a chair in the shape of a nude woman with arms extended and asked Rendón to sit in it. Highly offended, Rendón left. Rendón was further scandalized when the members, all young men, "started to drink beer and smoke pot." According to Ortega, "Henry would have nothing to do with impropriety of that nature, especially when they were carving santos. I used to tell him, `But Henry, [the carver of the chair] is a Presbyterian. He doesn't like santos!' `I know, but the rest are supposed to be good Catholics!' [Rendón] replied with a very serious demeanor."[12] For Rendón, the compulsion to carve abstract and figurative pieces, especially nudes, along with religious images could not coexist.

STYLE

Rendón's manner of carving saints often elicits pleasurable comments from observers. Luis Tapia once referred to Rendón as "the cosmic santero," because of his constant depiction of images with wide-open eyes. A prolific collector of folk art considers Rendón's saints among "the most innovative within the contemporary Hispanic santero tradition. . . . their faces have eyes that are round and popeyed with long lashes, and they are brightly colored."[13]

No matter what color Rendón chose to paint the faces of his images, he always clearly articulated the whites of his santos' eyes. Usually, he outlined them with black eyelashes and heavy eyebrows, and he gave his saints piercing dark eyes. The santos portrayed an innocence that was only accentuated by cheerful smiles, bright clothing, iconographic attributes, and a frontal, "friendly" stance (i.e., tilted head, outstretched arms).

Rather than brooding, bloody saints, such as those found in moradas, Enrique Rendón's images have a lighthearted quality. The carver himself often smiled when he talked about his "statues." They resemble figures from animation cels and other forms of popular culture as much as they do religious folk art found in the local Spanish colonial churches. Where many contemporary santeros favor discussions about the aesthetic form of their work, its political implications, or its iconographic integrity, Rendón preferred to talk about the particular materials that made up his saints—the cottonwood and aspen logs, plastic rosaries, straw hat key chains, mass-produced pine bases, and so forth that together formed the images he loved and devoted his life to. It was not the idea of santos that interested Rendón, but the santos themselves.

PATRONS

Despite having little outlet for the sale of his santos in public markets, Rendón produced crafts for what Michael Owen Jones calls "at least two major consumer publics"—the local people from Velarde with whom Rendón interacted and shared common experiences and an outside clientele whom Rendón did not know and for whom he made a rather different product.[14] A third group of patrons Rendón also served included an outside clientele whom he did get to know and for whom he made a product similar to that which he made for local people.

The craftsman-client relationships Rendón had with his patrons were always dyadic. Local people approached Rendón directly at his house, encountering him in a room that held a three-tiered metal cart on which the carver displayed his works. And Rendón visited Elma Bal, owner of Potrero's Trading Post in Chimayó, who commissioned images from Rendón to sell to outside patrons.

With only a few variations, the contractual agreements between Rendón and his patrons fell within sociologist Louis Chiaramonte's framework of specified and open transactions, in which the distinguishing feature was whether the terms were named before the job was started (specified) or after it had been completed (open). These terms were always defined in the client's approach to the craftsman—indirect for open transactions and direct for those specified.[15] In different circumstances in Velarde, contractual agreements with local people and outsiders took on each of these forms. An example of one open contract with a local patron, a "lady down the road" whose name Rendón forgot, follows. The woman stopped at the wood-carvers's house, looking to buy a wooden santo.

> LBK: Did she stop by or call you?
>
> ER: No, she stopped by and . . . she's been, eh, saying she wanted some—statues—
>
> LBK: Uh huh.
>
> ER: But then, she'd like—she wanted a crucifix/image of Christ on the Cross, referred to locally as a Christ. . . .
>
> LBK: She did?
>
> ER: Yeah, but her, he—her husband doesn't like, you know, like—things that like turn blooden or something . . . (laughs)
>
> LBK: (laughs) He thinks what?
>
> ER: Like blood, you know?
>
> LBK: Oh he doesn't like the blood.
>
> ER: Yeah, no. . . . and—then she saw San Antonio and said, "Le'me—can I take him to church with (me?)" "Yeah," I said. "Take him."
>
> LBK: Uh huh.

ER: And then she said, "Well for sure I want Santa Teresa" . . . but then . . . she came yesterday back . . .

LBK: Yeah—

ER: And she said, "And now I want to take both."

Rendón and I laughed at how his customer depleted him of his santos. But he then jovially countered, "That's what they're for, no?" The santos were there, in the living room, to be sold.

As my conversation with Rendón shows, the woman who came to see him sought a santo produced with the carver's expertise but did not know exactly the type of image she wanted nor the extent to which the carver would help her. As a result, she engaged in a "warming-up period" of conversation and initiated an indirect approach.[16] The woman thought she might like a Cristo, but the ones on display in the front room were decorated with more blood than her husband would have liked. Therefore, she was unable to buy one. The woman persisted in her quest for a santo, however, but still in an open manner. She asked to bring one of the saints already on display in Rendón's house to church without expressly articulating her intentions to buy it. In her appeal to "test out the saint," to place it in a religious setting, the woman undercommunicated Rendón's role as craftsman and she overcommunicated his role as community member. She appealed to the carver's sensitivity to the spiritual role of santos. Rendón obliged the woman's indirect request, and the result was a direct order, "for sure," for another santo, an image of Santa Teresa del Niño (Saint Theresa of the Child Jesus).

Although a sales transaction was made, it did not negate the deep meaning the carving had for the craftsman and his patron. The two attended closely to iconographic details of the Santa Teresa. Rendón arranged the saints' attributes—black and white nun's garb, with cloak, a cross and flowers—according to his neighbor's desires as well as to the figures illustrated in a brightly colored children's picture book of saints that shop owner Elma Bal first introduced him to. And Rendón and his neighbor negotiated a religious and personal significance for the santo along with a commercial value. Rendón did not clarify in his story why the woman wanted the saint—either to decorate her living room or to use in prayer—but he did emphasize the modification and articulation of iconographic details. For Rendón as well as for his patron, religion, spirituality, aesthetics, and the market coexisted.

Like the Oviedos, Rendón used his home as a display space. However, in contrast to the clarity of presentation and uniform ideology present at the Oviedos', the arrangement of santos at Rendón's house was practical; as a result, the santos had a more opaque meaning. Rendón set most of his santos on a cart in his living room, the area first entered from outside, and where he conducted most of his business. But he also placed santos in other parts of the house, particularly in his bedroom, where he put carvings on top of the television set, a table, and the coal stove. Because no clear separation of viewing space existed for visitors, except for the division of the rooms themselves, Rendón could take interested guests throughout the house to see either what he happened to be working on or the images he was particularly fond of. Many of the santos throughout the house were for sale. Yet although they were for sale, the santos also had religious value for the maker.

Elma Bal remembers a touching story Rendón told her that illustrates how he relied on his carvings for religious and economic sustenance. Enrique

OVERLEAF

Left

Fig. 106. *New Picture Book of Saints. Illustrated Lives of the Saints for Young and Old,* by Rev. Lawrence G. Lovasik, S.V.D. Courtesy Catholic Book Publishing, New York. Copies of this book, which Rendón relied heavily on for iconographic information about saints, are available in great quantity at Potrero Trading Post. Collection: Gene Autry Western Heritage Museum. Gift of Laurie Beth Kalb. Photo: Susan Einstein.

Right

Fig. 107. Bulto of San Miguel Arcángel, 1990, by Alcario Otero. Collection: Charles M. Carrillo. Photo: Mary Peck.

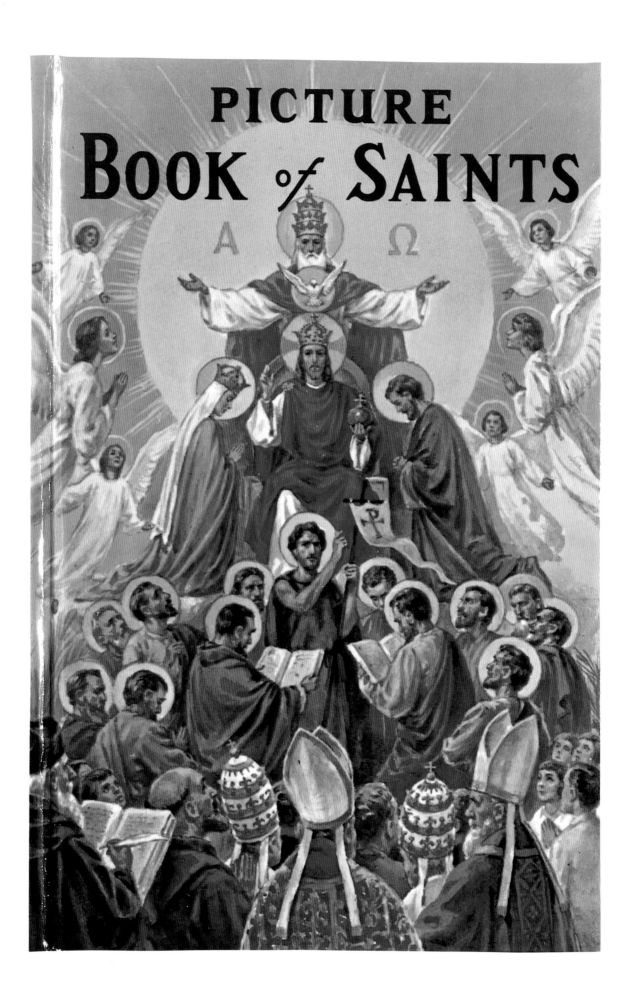

PICTURE
BOOK of SAINTS

Rendón stopped by Potrero's store one day to deliver a santo to Elma Bal for her to sell in her shop. He had just come from Santa Fe, where his first wife was in the hospital, and he was crying. Elma Bal asked Rendón how his wife was doing and he answered, "she's pretty sick." Rendón explained that he had been with his wife all day and was holding her hand. As he was leaving the hospital, he met an old lady who told him to "just let go of [his] wife. If the Lord needed her more than [Rendón, he] should let her go." After he arrived home, took a shower, and prepared to go back to the hospital to see his wife again, Rendón kneeled down in front of his santos. He told the Lord, "If you need her more than me, I will let her go." That night, when Rendón returned to the hospital, he let go of his wife's hand, and she died that evening."

When he sold his images from his home, Rendón made it a policy not to accept payment for santos until they were complete. Pointing to the unfinished carving of Santa Teresa he began work on for his neighbor, he discussed his payment procedure:

LBK: Well…. Did she pay you already?

ER: No.

LBK: When it's done?

ER: No. She will pay me when… I like them pay me when it's—

LBK: When it's finished?

ER: Finished. That way if they, if they like it, they pay me…. I don't want … I don't like to take money, you know,…before.

Less fiscally sophisticated than, say, Marco Oviedo, who requests a deposit before beginning work on a commission, Enrique Rendón nonetheless engaged in complex sales negotiations.

Sales arrangements, on the other hand, which Rendón made with Elma Bal of Potrero's Trading Post in Chimayó were far less complicated than those he conducted from his home. To begin with, when Rendón first met Elma Bal in the early 1980s, he was not necessarily even interested in selling his saints. He made a lot of images and gave them away; he had not yet begun to sell santos from his home. Elma Bal recalls that Rendón "loved the Penitentes. He just loved to make the santos." As Elma Bal, and now her son Raymond, do with other carvers whose work they especially like, including Alcario Otero and Victor Goler, she invited Rendón to make some santos for her shop. At first, she did not commission the wood-carver per se; she simply offered him a new venue for display, and the venue happened to be a market. According to Elma Bal, this encouraged Rendón a lot. Eventually, people noticed the carvings and began to order them.

Once a market interest developed for Rendón's work, Elma Bal began to take his santos on consignment. If the work sold, she paid the carver. If it did not sell, neither the shop owner nor the wood-carver profited. Eventually, with Rendón's rising popularity, Elma Bal commissioned him. She asked him directly to produce a certain number and style of saints, which she bought and then resold.

Among the most common saints Elma Bal requested was an image of San Cajetán, defined locally as the patron saint of law, and by dictionaries and scholarly literature as the patron saint of gamblers and pawn shops.[17] She asked that the carvings remain unpainted, which left them with much less iconographic detail. According to Bal, "Customers prefer[red] unpainted ones." Rendón decorated his unpainted images of San Cajetán with iconographic attributes, but unlike the painted santos, these were merely chipped or engraved into the wood. They did not have the color differentiation or miniature plastic accessories that Rendón used for his other saints.

In a remarkably similar way, the form, decoration, and marketing of Rendón's San Cajetáns paralleled those of Córdovan José Dolores López's images from the 1920s and 1930s craft revival. Both Rendón and López produced their santos commercially. In both cases, the craftsmen used the chip-carving style because it conformed to outside aesthetics.[18] Because of the chip-carving style's popularity with the market, it also generated an element of competition in the carvers' works. Jealousy first arose among Córdova wood-carvers because of the Anglos' economic encouragement "to produce more goods in less time for higher profits."[19] It also occurred when Rendón produced his carvings exclusively in response to market tastes. As Elma Bal, for example, mentioned how Rendón made copies of San Cajetán, she also explained how they did not compare with her husband's images of the same saint. Robert Bal, Elma's husband, is a highly talented wood-carver who produces very detailed images of saints. Elma's competitive attitude is especially noteworthy because Robert pursues wood carving as an avocation rather than as a profession.

Sometimes Rendón and Elma Bal redefined the formal businesslike nature of their transactions. During one interview, Rendón continuously showed me the children's picture books of saints and catalogues of religious paraphernalia that Elma Bal introduced him to. Rendón referred to these books for models of many of the santos he carved—San Martín de Porres, for example, and Santa Teresa del Niño, Santa Teresa de Avila, San Francisco de Asís, San Antonio, and Nuestra Señora de Guadalupe, along with San Cajetán. Elma Bal's gift of the books and catalogues openly encouraged Rendón to continue carving. Thanks to the books, he had models for a wide range of saints. Thus, he could meet the specific needs of his patrons.

Rendón claimed that before he met Elma Bal and began to copy saints from popular picture books, he used missal books, those official liturgical books of Roman Catholic rites used by priests to celebrate mass throughout the year. Perhaps because the corpus of religious figures in missal books is so small—often limited to Apostles (Rendón claimed to have only occasionally found depictions of saints)—he switched over to Elma Bal's picture books completely and stopped using any liturgical prototypes.

Rendón reflected on the difference between his images and those in churches by saying, "Well I guess every . . . a lot of people have a different style, I don't know why but . . . but—" and explained that although no one taught him to carve, he began his craft by going to see santos in galleries. The santos Rendón saw in galleries represented examples of Spanish colonial folk images that once furnished village chapels and that today have been largely replaced by mass-produced santos made with plaster of Paris or lead.

The sources Rendón used, children's picture books of saints and Spanish colonial santos, differ from the prints and other religious art officially sanctioned by the Catholic church. But the combination itself—of popular and folk sources—distinguished Rendón from many contemporary carvers in search of a "pure," "authentic" folk tradition. Unlike others, such as Félix López, Marco and Patricia Oviedo, and José Benjamín López, for example, who mix local clays to make natural pigments, Enrique Rendón used acrylics and store-bought wa-

OVERLEAF

Left

Fig. 108. Spanish colonial revival–style door, 1991, by Lawrence Quintana. Today, most unpainted, chip-carved santos are produced by Córdova descendants of José Dolores López. The artist who made this door, Lawrence Quintana of Santa Fe, has no familial relationship to the Córdova wood-carvers. Although Córdova carvers produce many beautiful chip-carved images of saints, this is the first replica of doors by José Dolores López. The scalloped edges, S shapes at the top, leaves and birds on the bottom, and even the incised initials at the center are direct copies of López's work. Collection: Gene Autry Western Heritage Museum. Photo: Susan Einstein.

Right

Fig. 109. Bulto of Nuestra Señora de Guadalupe, 1991, by Félix López. Blue ribbon for first place in bulto category, 1991 Spanish Market, cottonwood or aspen, natural pigments, straw inlay, piñon sap and grain alcohol varnish. Collection: Gene Autry Western Heritage Museum. Photo: Susan Einstein.

tercolors to color his carvings. Further, Rendón's reliance on mass-produced church literature for references contrasted sharply with the Oviedos', Benjamín López's, and other carvers' dependence on museum exhibition catalogues and fine-art books for information.

Rather than assume an artistic role or attempt to replicate the past, Rendón perpetuated tradition by working with present-day materials and sources. He purchased religious goods and santo ornaments from mail-order catalogues and read Marvel comic books about saints. He also relied on plaster-of-Paris santos as models for his carvings. Although the carver used these statues as models, he also gave them religious value. Displayed neatly on a table in a storage room of his house appeared a couple of used candles in front of at least two plaster images. One of these plaster images was a gift from Zoraida Ortega.

For Enrique Rendón, authenticity was not elusive. It did not stand outside of itself. Instead, it was part of the santero's lived experience. Whereas, for example, Marco and Patricia Oviedo invited visitors into the environment they created for spectators and guests, Enrique Rendón made room for visitors in a world that had little to do with them. The santos he made commemorated attachments to his daily life and were continuous with the larger tradition of producing Hispano Catholic religious images. Mutual admiration of santos formed the basis of Rendón's many friendships with researchers, patrons, and casual visitors. Through making and selling santos, Rendón created and enhanced for himself rich social connections.[20]

MAKING SAINTS

The tools Rendón used to carve his santos resemble those of other contemporary carvers. His basic repertoire consisted of a handsaw for cutting a block of wood from a tree trunk, generally cottonwood or aspen; a pocketknife for shaping the general form of the body; a variety of chisels for carving the details such as the face, hands, and dress; a mallet for pounding the wood, which usually meant securing two pieces of wood joined by dowels; a drill for setting holes for dowels; and an electric sander—although, according to Rendón, "they don't last long. Better to do it by hand."

Rendón carefully chose two different verbs when he explained the way he used his tools. "Shaping" was reserved for coarse work and "carving" for refinement. This choice of terms resembles a similar distinction Luis Tapia once made. In the early 1980s, Tapia distinguished the production of small pieces, usually santos, as "carving," and the production of large pieces, those "get[ting] on a large scale, like twenty inches," as "sculpting, . . . and that's a lot different." Tapia's large pieces, his "sculptures," were not ordinarily images of saints. Rather, they were his abstract or figurative carvings, the latter often depicting elongated, shapely, sensuous women. Although the words *shaping, carving,* and *sculpting* had slightly different meanings for Rendón and Tapia, the fact that both had specific uses for them suggests that both made aesthetic distinctions.

Enrique Rendón's basic craft materials included a rich mix of both natural resources and manufactured miniature souvenirs. Most often, the santero used aspen for his carving, but he also relied on local milled lumber and cottonwood, which he collected along the nearby Rio Grande. Rendón tended to his wood in a way that santeros have done for the last two hundred years. He attempted to get dry wood, which he then kept inside to keep from cracking. But he also

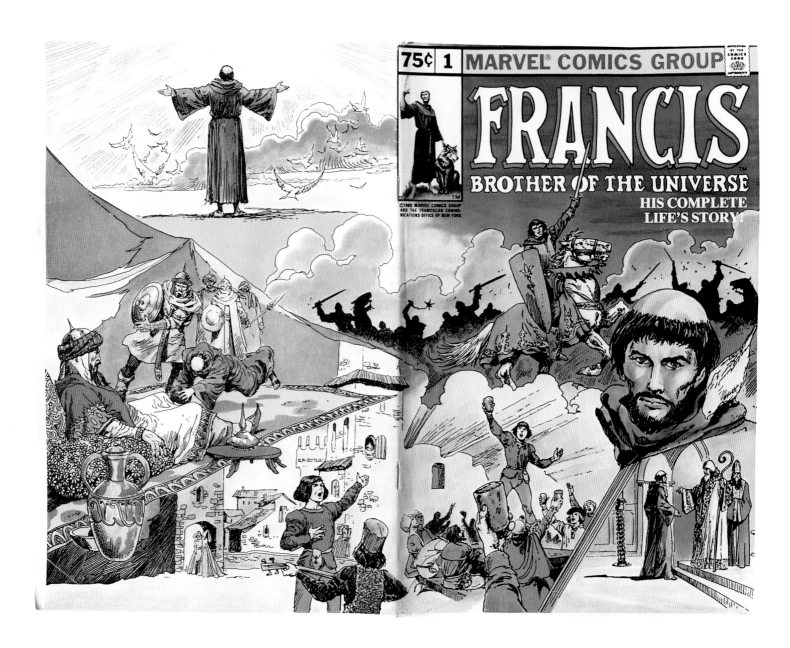

Fig. 110. Marvel comic book, *Francis. Brother of the Universe. His Complete Life's Story.* This is one of many popular culture forms Rendón relied on for making santos. Anonymous collection. Photo: Mary Peck.

Fig. 111. Interior, La Capilla del Santo Niño de Atocha (Chapel of the Holy Child of Atocha), Chimayó, 1991. Since at least the beginning of the twentieth century, this chapel has been owned and cared for by a local Hispano family. All the santos are made of plaster of Paris, with the exception of a bulto of San Antonio de Padua (Saint Anthony of Padua), made by Enrique Rendón, and located on the far left of the table next to the altar. Unlike other more self-consciously artistic contemporary santos, this wooden image of San Antonio is indistinguishable from the chapel's mass-produced saints. Courtesy Susana Duran. Photo: Mary Peck.

Fig. 112. Bulto of Kateri Tekakwitha, 1986, by Enrique Rendón, cottonwood or aspen, pine, sawdust, paint, feathers, leather, miniature basket, silk flowers, rocks. Collection: Gene Autry Western Heritage Museum. Gift of Robert and Ruth Vogele. Photo: Susan Einstein.

Kateri Tekakewitha

gathered green wood, which he stored until it was sufficiently dry for carving. In order for green wood to dry faster, Rendón, like other santeros, took the bark off the wood, peeling it with a hatchet, and then cut the log in half with an axe. The log still needed a year to dry sufficiently, and he kept it out of direct sunlight, to avoid cracks. Often, the wood-carver had to chop off the ends of a dried log before he could achieve a piece of wood for carving.

Like most santeros, Rendón coated his carvings with gesso before he applied paint to them. Generally, the carver used store-bought gesso, although at least one source describes the gesso Rendón used as a homemade mixture of flour, paste, and water.[21] All the colors Rendón used to paint his santos resembled the bright and cheery shades displayed in his picture books of saints and comics.

Although conscientious about depicting accurate iconographic detail, Rendón almost never carved any of the saints' attributes. Rather, he created attributes from miniatures gathered from various sources. Some of these consisted of objects from nature—small sticks, cacti, and flat rocks. Other manufactured miniatures included key chains with little straw hats attached to them, small plastic rosaries, miniature religious medals, tiny straw baskets, wooden buckets, feathers, and artificial flowers. As with the natural materials, Rendón kept the mass-produced items in good order, storing many of them in plastic bags. The manufactured objects had a multitude of uses. For example, Rendón used the straw hats from the key chains as head coverings for santos, particularly San Ysidro Labrador, patron saint of farmers. He attached feathers to leather headbands worn by his carvings of the Mohawk saint Kateri Tekakwitha. He used his miniature baskets and wood buckets as containers to be held by many

Fig. 113. Enrique Rendón's carved wooden heads for santos, stored in plastic bucket, Velarde, 1985. Photo: Laurie Beth Kalb.

of his santos, including the patron of pilgrimages, Santo Niño de Atocha, San Ysidro Labradór, and Kateri Tekakwitha.

Rendón not only organized and used his miniatures well but also literally gathered them in bulk, often making large purchases from arts-and-crafts supply stores. At times he had such a large horde of small ornaments that the quantity caricatured the miniature size of the objects. The carver joked about this irony. After once giving me a little straw hat from a large plastic bag filled with them, Rendón playfully commented, "You never know when you're going to be able to find these things, so I always buy a lot."

Just as Rendón stocked up on "attributes," so did he maintain an adequate cache of body parts for his santos. Rendón made a large group of spare carved wooden heads, ready to be dowelled into torsos. He varied the expressions on the faces of these heads along with their size, but he carved them in a similar form so he could attach them to different wooden bodies. Rendón stored these heads in a white plastic bucket.

COLLECTING

Enrique Rendón not only sold his work to collectors, he was a collector himself. He relished small things, such as his miniatures of religious paraphernalia, and he amused himself by gathering them. However, unlike art collectors, Rendón did not separate the usefulness of his collections from his admiration of them. In fact, it was precisely the functional possibilities of the small items he gathered that caused Rendón joy. For Rendón, collecting plastic trinkets and small objects from nature was not an end in itself, it was a means to making good santos.

According to folklorist Susan Stewart, capitalism has witnessed a transformation in daily life from industrial production to spectacle. Objects once produced for use decreased in size and became toys as the market for full-sized goods diminished due to changes in the economic system. Subsequently, as the demand for miniatures increased, they were no longer models. Rather, they became souvenirs of a mode of consumption that is now extinct, passing into the realm of sheer "amusements."[22]

Enrique Rendón's miniatures, or souvenirs, undoubtedly entertained him. He enjoyed showing them to me as much as he liked displaying the santos he had for sale. However, Rendón did not gather miniatures for exhibiting. Rather, he used them as iconographic attributes for santos and thereby changed their significance from something sentimental to something immediately relevant. Indeed, Rendón transformed souvenirs into functional items. As Nelson Graburn writes about the way the collection of foreign, exotic arts represents a "nostalgic input of the handmade in a 'plastic world,'" one could argue that Rendón, a traditional artist, engaged in the nostalgic input of the plastic in a handmade world.[23]

The objects Rendón selected for his saints and his very particular range of saintly subjects reflected his experiences. Like the patrons who visited him from other places, Enrique Rendón liked to travel. He journeyed by bus to Mexico City. He also drove to Utah, where his brother Leo lives, and to other Southwestern cities. On returning from a trip to Mexico City, after making a pilgrimage to the shrine of Our Lady of Guadalupe on her feast day (12 December), Rendón showed me the articles of commemoration he gathered. They included family snapshots and photographs of religious images—churches, pictures of Christ, and various saints. Rendón also brought back "posters" (postcards) of religious images and a *caicomania* (decal) of a very bloody Christ. Rendón planned to use these souvenirs as models for his own saints.

Enrique Rendón's travels and adventures always had religious import. His sister, Dulcinea López compared the range of her hobbies—bowling, camping, bingo, and gambling in Las Vegas—to those of her late brother—praying and the morada. Among the souvenirs Rendón prized most was what he called a "natural" wooden cross he once discovered lying on the road near his house. The "artifact," a thick tree branch with a second branch attached and extended in a perpendicular angle like a Catholic cross, held much significance for the carver because of its shape and the fact that he found it. Rendón affixed a rawhide loop onto the top of the "cross," hanging it on his living room wall. During each visit I made to the house, Rendón related how he came upon the cross and that many visitors wanted to buy it, but that he refused to sell it. A family member subsequently saved the cross, like other fragments of Rendón's santo activities. The object acquired meaning through Rendón's story about it, exemplifying how the santero was a true collector and tourist of his own surroundings.

TERMS AND REPERTOIRE

Although Rendón called himself a santero, a maker of santos, he casually used the English, secular term *statues* when referring to the religious images he carved. Manufacturers and members of the local community apply the term to mass-produced, plaster-of-Paris, religious figures, used widely in churches, private altars, and other sacred spaces. The popular association between the term *statue* and religious article at first seems ironic—to use a secular word for a sacred object; however, if one considers the "arty by wordiness" now linked with retablos and bultos, the popular use of statue makes perfect functional sense.[24] If, on the other hand, one draws a historical parallel for religious and secular terms attached to carved images of saints, the situation is reversed. In his study of José Dolores López, influential image-carver of the early-twentieth-century craft revival, Charles Briggs relates that when López spoke among his relatives and friends about his chip-carved images of saints, he used the term *monos*, not santos. Unlike Rendón, whose secular term for his images connoted religious significance, López's use of *monos* asserted a lack of piety. According to López, the commercial "santos he was making weren't from the heart."[25] Rendón's, on the other hand, were spiritual.

Eulogio Ortega wondered one evening about the nature of contemporary santos. First, he wanted to know why people who were not religious and who came from other parts of the country bought santos and, then, whether the santos had any inherent spiritual value anyway, as they were "merely copies of what was done before." Almost as if to present an exception to his own critical rule about the nature of contemporary santos, Ortega brought out an early image by Rendón, a San Antonio dated 1976. He and I delighted in this piece, which was iconographically sophisticated—a young man in the particularly Mexican and New Mexican depiction of a blue, rather than the brown or gray of European usage, robe (in honor of the Immaculate Conception of Mary, whose primary color is blue), holding a Christ Child.[26] On the other hand, its form was what Ortega called "primitive" and what folklorists might call conventional, geometric, "perfected" or "folk"—with the baby in San Antonio's arms lying flat instead of curled up, and the arms of San Antonio outstretched perfectly straight instead of wrapped around the baby.[27] According to Ortega, Rendón's work "came directly from the spirit and was not a copy of anything." In this way, Rendón's work was more like the older colonial santos than the modern replications. Ortega reasoned that the older santos were also "carved from the spirit and didn't follow any model." The settlers who came to New Mexico had nothing but "self-reliance."

Although he carved and decorated each of his santos individually, an element of assembly-line manufacture prevailed in Rendón's saint making. One could say that like Marco Oviedo, Enrique Rendón produced a finite "line" of santos. His santos were not replicas of Spanish colonial images. In fact, many of the subjects he carved were never even common in northern New Mexico. Ortega recalls that "Henry carved santos that I have never heard of."[28] Still, Rendón produced a set repertoire of various subjects that became familiar to his patrons and that he was apt to reproduce. Some of these included santos well known to New Mexicans, such as San Antonio, San Francisco, San Ysidro Labrádor, and Nuestra Señora de Guadalupe.

Rendón's most unusual santo forms were his retablos. Although retablos, or wood-panel paintings, are as traditional a New Mexico santo type as three-dimensional bultos, the form of Rendón's retablos deviated from the norm. Most Spanish colonial panels were painted on flat surfaces, usually pine, and noted for their total lack of three-dimensional illusion.[29] Rendón painted his retablos on semiround pieces of bark from Taos cottonwood trees, sculpting them in bas-relief.

One could argue that Rendón's bas-relief paintings had prototypes in a rare form of retablo dating from the eighteenth and early nineteenth centuries. These were wood panels built up with layers of wet gesso, carved out in design, and painted on the surface. However, these works were often less skillfully executed than the flat painted panels and considered "childlike" in form.[30] Rendón's retablos, on the other hand, were highly refined, with attention to figures' physical proportions and iconographic detail. They also constituted relatively late developments in the wood-carver's repertoire, the first examples dating from the early 1980s. He used the same process as on the old gesso relief panels—sawing off a piece of wood, applying layers of gesso, carving out the image, and painting it. But Rendón seemed to work on these paintings continuously with an apparent intention of perfecting the form.

Rendón showed me four images he painted on the Taos bark—Santo Niño de Atocha, San Francisco, San Antonio, and Kateri Tekakwitha. Both the Santo Niño and the San Francisco were dated 1982. All four retablos remained on view in Rendón's home at least through 1985. Apparently, they were not among his most marketable saints.

One of Rendón's retablos, of Santo Niño de Atocha, hung from a hook against one of the living room walls. It represented the flattest piece of bark. The other three panels, all of which were curved, were attached to pine bases. They represented a truly intermediate form between panel paintings and freestanding bultos. However, unlike a transition suggested by Yvonne Lange, in which the embellishments on Spanish colonial retablos became superfluous as santeros shifted from painting panels to carving "unencumbered" bultos, the very bases of Rendón's bark paintings, which turn them from retablos into freestanding bultos, became laden down over time.[31]

Gradually, Rendón added decorations and religious accoutrements to the bases, which he had at first kept clean. On the base of the San Antonio image, for example, Rendón placed two votive candles, which emphasized the

SaN ANTONio
De Padua

<Fig. 114. Bulto of San Antonio de Padua, 1976, by Enrique Rendón. According to Robert and Ruth Vogele, who received this santo as a gift from Rendón, the artist claimed that this was his first carving. Collection: Gene Autry Western Heritage Museum. Gift of Robert and Ruth Vogele. Photo: Susan Einstein.

Fig. 115. Home display of Raymond Smith collection, including bas-relief retablo by Enrique Rendón, Velarde, 1992. Smith, owner of local businesses in Española and Santa Fe, collects a wide assortment of antiques, Indian pottery, and contemporary New Mexico santos. In one room of his house, he and his wife, Viola, display the family collection in a museumized setting, with old tools hung separately on the wall, and santos and pottery placed carefully on shelves. This photograph shows the following bultos and retablos: (left to right) San Juan Nepomuceno (Saint John Nepomuk), n.d, and Santa Rita de Cascia (Saint Rita of Cascia), 1978, by Horacio Valdez; Kateri Tekakwitha, 1981, by Enrique Rendón; and San Santiago, 1985, by Johnny Martínez and Max Roybal. Rendón acquired the round piece of wood for his retablo from Taos Pueblo craftspeople. Courtesy Raymond and Viola Smith. Photo: Mary Peck.

spiritual value of the form. On the base of the retablo of San Francisco, Rendón eventually added free-standing figures of a lamb and a burro. Rendón enhanced the three-dimensional quality of these animals by simulating a fur texture on the body surfaces. He achieved this by applying Elmer's glue to the wood surface, then adding sawdust, a coat of gesso, and finally, paint. Visually, the addition of free-standing animals, especially with a textured surface, emphasized a transformation of the retablo form into statue form.

Other New Mexico animal carvers, especially Felipe Archuleta and his followers, also simulated fur textures on their images of beasts. However, it is unlikely that Rendón knew the carvers who practiced these methods. Animal wood-carvers such as Archuleta did not ordinarily produce santos. Still, the similarity of method suggests that Rendón must have had some exposure to New Mexico animal carvings. In 1979, the Albuquerque Museum included Rendón's and Archuleta's work along with art by other contemporary Hispano artists in the exhibition "One Space/Three Visions."[32] More often than not, however, museums and galleries do not exhibit animal carvings and santos together.

Along with making innovative retablos, Rendón incorporated new materials, specifically Indian ones, into his own Hispano-Catholic tradition. Rendón took the wood to make his semiround retablos from the bark of trees Taos Indians use to make drums. The bark was not merely Indian, but Indian material used for making sacred Indian craft drums, which, like santos, are for sale. Although Rendón's use of sacred Indian material served the production of a purely Catholic image and form and hence was not "really assimilated," I cannot help but wonder why the santero had the material of religious drums, which are also commercial, in mind for his carving and painting.[33] Perhaps the true syncretism between the Taos wood and the Spanish santo was the blend of commerce and religion rather than an exclusive religious meaning. Another major aspect to this mixture may have had to do with Rendón's wife, Margaret. A Spanish santo made of sacred Indian materials is a lovely symbol of the union between a Hispano wood-carver and his Indian wife.

Rendón's syncretic tendencies extended not only to the forms of his santos but to their subjects. Rendón favored the image of San Martín de Porres, as he did that of Kateri Tekakwitha. According to *Attwater's Dictionary of Saints*, San Martín was a Dominican laybrother, born in Lima, Peru.[34] He was a mulatto, born of a Spanish *hidalgo* (nobleman) and an Indian woman from Panama. He had many jobs in the Dominican friary, among them barber, farm laborer, and infirmarian, and he was also helpful in solving people's delicate personal affairs. In the United States, Martín de Porres has been adopted as patron saint of work for interracial justice and harmony. Rendón produced more santos with brown skin—representing mulattos—than any other contemporary santero. His brown-skinned santos included Kateri Tekakwitha; St. Martín de Porres; the Guatemalan image of Christ on the Cross, Nuestro Señor de Esquípulas; and a brown-faced Mexican invocation of the Virgin, Nuestra Señora de Guadalupe.

When producing santos, Rendón mixed his attention to iconographic detail with a penchant for experimenting with craftsmanship. As he did with his retablo of St. Francis, Rendón gradually embellished his bultos of San Martín de Porres with animal figures placed on the santo's base. He carved a small gray mouse sneaking up to a bowl of food ostensibly left for a white dove. Rendón rendered the food by gluing pieces of Rice Crispies cereal into a wooden bowl. This humorous portrayal fits perfectly well with the legend that San Martín "had a great concern for animals, including vermin, about which engaging tales are told."[35]

Unlike other carvers, such as Marco Oviedo, Luis Tapia, and Luisito Luján, who expanded their repertoires by inventing their own saints or carving subjects from the Old Testament, Rendón only made images that exist in the Catholic hagiography. He was motivated by a deep religious exploration of subject matter. Whereas, for example, Marco Oviedo studies and copies tradition, Rendón lived it. He was never alienated from his community or his faith. He was a devout Catholic who, as Eulogio Ortega explains, "grew up with the santos in the different moradas. Cristos that were awe inspiring. Not pretty santos that many of us carve."[36] The power of his faith gave Rendón the freedom to produce unusual santos that reflected his own personal preferences and experiences.

RENDÓN AS *HERMANO MAYOR*

Enrique Rendón experimented with the form, style, and subject of his santos at home, but he never placed any of his carvings in the Lyden morada, where he performed his duties as *hermano mayor* of the local chapter of the Brotherhood of Our Father Jesus. As *hermano mayor*, he served as administrator, arbiter, and overseer of all rituals as well as the morada's chief representative in council affairs and in dealings with priests and various outsiders.[37] His administrative tasks revolved around a commitment to spiritual discipline and the expression of religious devotion. They had little to do with the making of art.

Rendón held the elected position of *hermano mayor* consecutively for the last eight years of his life. He took his job very seriously. Once a man be-

Fig. 116. Bulto of San Martín de Porres (Saint Martin of Porres), 1983, by Enrique Rendón, cottonwood, pine, acrylics, straw, pipe cleaners, Rice Crispies cereal. Collection: Gene Autry Western Heritage Museum. Gift of Robert and Ruth Vogele. Photo: Susan Einstein.

ST. Martin
de Porres

comes an *hermano,* he is a life-long member, whether or not he participates in the rituals. Rendón, or "'Mano Henry" as the brothers called him, felt responsible for all the other *hermanos.* He did not appreciate the fact that some dropped out and never returned.

Rendón took responsibility for the care of santos in the morada. Because of theft and vandalism, by art collectors and others, the brothers distributed many of the morada's very old santos throughout their homes. They only brought these images to the morada during Lent and Holy Week. Rendón himself took santos loaned to the morada by a local family home with him in the evenings.[38]

In each morada, the corpus of santos required for Holy Week observances includes the principal figures of the Passion—the Nazarene Christ (Man of Sorrows); Cristo Crucificado (Christ Crucified), often jointed to allow removal from the Cross on Good Friday; Our Lady of Sorrows; St. John the Disciple; and St. Veronica.[39] Because images must be life-sized for use in the Passion Play, *hermanos* use older santos, dating from the Spanish colonial era and the mid-nineteenth century. Mass-produced plaster-of-Paris images, first introduced to the region in the late nineteenth century, also appear in moradas; however, their height, which averages between one to two feet, precludes their use in Holy Week rituals.

When Horacio Valdez was active in the Lyden morada, the brothers recognized his masterful wood-carving skills, claiming two pieces in their holdings. These include a bulto of San José, the morada's patron saint, purchased by the brothers, and a Cristo, donated by Valdez. One brother notes a large discrepancy between the recognition the brothers gave Valdez and Rendón as woodcarvers. They raised a sizable sum to buy a piece from Valdez, but many paid no attention at all to Rendón's wood carving. According to this brother, it seemed natural that Valdez made santos. He was a carpenter by trade. With Rendón, there was no logical progression. Further, Valdez was more assertive and "more generous" with his work. He donated a piece to the morada; 'Mano Henry' did not. Apparently, Rendón brought his santos to the morada on an informal basis, to show people what he was doing, but he did not try to incorporate them into his dealings with the brotherhood.

As the brother reflects on the santos produced by Valdez and Rendón, he ponders the fact that they are given no particular notice. The crucifix donated by Valdez has no special location in the morada. "You know what's amazing," he reports, "you can't hardly see where [the crucifix is] placed." As he talks about Rendón's wood carving, the brother almost apologetically confesses that he never really considered Rendón's work as art. For this brother, the morada had no artistic associations, therefore, Rendón's images had no recognizable artistic context. He began to view Rendón's images aesthetically after reading my exhibition catalogue that discussed them.[40] Still, he considers Rendón's work as separate from the art world. "Now," he says, "to have a piece of Henry's is just to have a piece of Henry."

Rendón's duties as *hermano mayor,* coupled with the perspective of his peer, suggest that it was not necessary for him to place his wood carvings in the meetinghouse. He may have been inspired to make saints because of a deep religious passion, but the other qualities associated with his carving—collecting ornaments, making money, and creating art—had little to do with the brotherhood. The morada, a place where rituals take place privately, is not a place for display. Further, as a place to practice humility in the eyes of God, it is not a place to celebrate one's own accomplishments. For the brother who reflects on

PREVIOUS PAGES

Left

Fig. 117. *Cristo of Nuestro Señor de Esquípulas* (Our Lord of Esquípulas), n.d., by Enrique Rendón. Anonymous collection. Photo: Mary Peck.

Right

Fig. 118. Display of bultos by Eulogio and Zoraida Ortega in their living room, Velarde, 1992. The combination of a doily placed in front of San Calletano, 1992, and a pedestal to hold Nuestra Señora de Guadalupe, 1989, suggests a mixture of religious devotion and attention to artful presentations that characterizes many contemporary santeros. Courtesy Eulogio and Zoraida Ortega. Photo: Mary Peck.

the carvings of his peers, the aesthetic function of santos is superfluous. In the morada, santos are a means to spiritual nourishment. That they are art is beside the point.

Although Enrique Rendón made little connection during his life between his wood carving and his position as *hermano mayor,* connections did exist between the members of the brotherhood and the contemporary New Mexico santo revival. Just before performing Las Tinieblas services at the morada in 1984, Rendón and his brothers obliged Eulogio and Zoraida Ortega by forming a procession to a private adobe chapel the couple had built in their front yard.[41] The brothers drove to the ditch on the Ortegas' property, left their cars, walked in a line carrying a lantern and cross, and sang *alabados* (religious hymns) until they reached the chapel.

The Ortegas based the style and function of their *capilla* (little chapel) on Spanish colonial private chapels, which were either built on the property or located in the homes of wealthy Hispano families. Especially in areas of highly dispersed settlement, chapels such as these frequently served extrafamilial ends as well as private needs. The skillfully crafted altar screen and bultos inside the Ortegas' chapel display the same elaborate provisions that many of the eighteenth- and nineteenth-century *capillas* showed.[42] They also resemble the traditional style of wood carvings that the Ortegas have sold at public markets. Still, at home, in their private spaces, these santos and their architectural structure remain sacred. Perhaps the production of religious art has been encouraged by the consumer-oriented curiosity of an outside world, but in the instance of the brothers' procession, the meaning of the santos for their makers was wholly spiritual and local. In this instance, any outside interest in the perpetuation of the art had only the power to reaffirm ties within the community.

COMMEMORATIONS

Since his death in 1987, Enrique Rendón's wood carvings have become valuable commodities in the folk-art world. Aficionados have replaced the gentle affection they once bestowed on Rendón's santos with a serious concern for the aesthetic worth and cultural integrity of such an important contemporary santero. Along with this change has come a rise in the cost of Rendón's santos. Simply put, the images are hard to find and even more difficult to buy.

However, although Rendón's wood carvings appear, albeit rarely, in high-priced art galleries, they are also cherished locally. Rendón's sister Dulcinea López and his widow Margaret have the wood-carver's images displayed in honored places in their homes. Dulcinea has placed three of the four santos she owns by her brother in a private altar in her bedroom, setting them in front of a vanity mirror and draping them with rosaries and other religious paraphernalia. She prays to these images every day. Margaret has hung Rendón's "natural" cross above the mantelpiece in her living room. It hangs on the wall with miniature Papago Indian bird baskets adorning each side. Until recently, Margaret also displayed two Rendón watercolor paintings, depicting the church in Velarde and the Lyden morada.

Fig. 119. Morada, Lyden, 1987.
Photo: Mary Peck.

Fig. 120. Eulogio and Zoradia Ortega at the
entrance to their private chapel, Velarde, 1992.
Photo: Mary Peck.

Fig. 122. Dulcinea López's home altar with three
bultos by her brother, Enrique Rendón, Velarde,
1991. Courtesy Dulcinea López. Photo: Mary
Peck.

Fig. 121. Interior of the Ortegas' chapel, Velarde, 1992. Courtesy Eulogio and Zoraida Ortega. Photo: Mary Peck.

196

Fig. 123. Mantelpiece with Enrique Rendón's "natural" cross adorned with miniature Papago bird baskets and four Rendón wood carvings, 1991. The bultos (left to right) are as follows: donkey in cart, Saint Jude of Thaddeus, Santa Theresa del Niño (Saint Theresa of the Child Jesus), and San Ysidro. Courtesy Margaret Gutierrez. Photo: Mary Peck.

Fig. 124. Watercolor of Velarde church, n.d., by
Enrique Rendón. Anonymous collection. Photo:
Mary Peck.

Visits with other community members who knew Rendón reveal an abundance of ways local people continue to experience the wood-carver. Larry Vigil, who grew up in the house behind Rendón's, has a miniature image of a guardian angel that the wood-carver made for him when, as a boy, he approached him with five dollars he had saved. Now a teenager, he still has the piece. Raymond Smith displays his Rendón santos amidst all the other local folk art he owns. Carefully arranged inside the Smith home, Rendón's santos are appreciated as they have always have been, but now with the added knowledge that art galleries are trying to sell them. Rendón's brother in the morada reflects on the life of the late wood-carver in terms of his local community. He derides what he calls the annual "Spanish Markup" (Spanish Market) and talks about how owning a piece by Rendón would equal having "a part of Henry" around. None of the community members who reflect on the late wood-carver are particularly concerned with the market interest in "Rendóns." Rather, they remember their neighbor and friend.

Ironically, Enrique Rendón came to epitomize authenticity in his very avoidance of it. By completely embracing the resources immediately available to him, including those from folk and popular sources, Rendón resisted "authentification." He relied on local materials and sources and rejected models of tradition invented by outsiders. Enrique Rendón ignored the abstract, generalized notions of "authenticity," "purity," and "folk art" espoused by some contemporary santeros and members of the elite Anglo art world. Rather than perpetuate a myth of tradition, Rendón created one as he went along.[43]

Fig. 125. Large Carretta de la Muerte, 1977, by Enrique Rendón, displayed in Smith home. Carretta de la Muerte by Horacio Valdez in background. Collection: Raymond and Viola Smith. Photo: Mary Peck.

5

CRAFTING DEVOTIONS, CRAFTING TRADITION

CONTEMPORARY NEW MEXICAN WOOD-CARVERS negotiate both the past and the present to craft their saints, creating their own notions of tradition. They rely on the cultural experiences of their ancestors, the dominant culture's museumizing of Hispano culture, and their own aesthetic, political, commercial, and religious goals to create cultural identity. For these carvers, santos and other wood carvings are a means of constructing tradition, while at the same time, for generations of New Mexican Hispanos, they are traditional objects of cultural and religious import. Some carvers, who make and sell wood carvings while ignoring others' self-conscious attempts at defining tradition, represent cultural authenticity for their protégés and peers.

Luis Tapia, who has found acceptance and success as a Chicano artist in the gallery world, calls the "art part of making santos" traditional. Marco Oviedo, who received a doctorate in animal sciences while establishing his santo-making and donkey-breeding business in Chimayó, claims that farming is traditional in the everyday life of santeros. José Benjamín López, who resists the art market but relies on the tenets of early-twentieth-century modernism, calls 1930s wood-carver Patrocinio Barela an organic abstractionist and considers him traditional. For these santeros and many of their associates, wooden santos and other carvings manifest a highly malleable form of tradition, of maintaining social relationships through time, that they use to achieve cultural expressive independence. Contemporary carvers rely on a multitude of retellings of their ethnic pasts and their individual experiences of those pasts to create new and relevant artistic expressions. Sometimes, in this process of "traditioning," carvers undergo such endless self-identification that they no longer refer to the past at all but rather to

Bulto of Nuestra Señora de los Dolores, 1990, by Gloria López Córdova. Detail of fig.129.

Fig. 126. Home altar in José Benjamín and Irene López's living room, Española, 1992. López and his relatives and friends built this stone addition onto his adobe living room. They fashioned the ceiling, of vigas (beams) and *latillas* (wood lath), after Spanish colonial architecture. The santos in this altar are as follows (left to right): life-sized Cristo by José Benjamín López; Madonna, from Mexico, artist unknown; bultos of San José (Saint Joseph) and La Virgen (the Virgin), ca. 1972, by José Benjamín López; Cristo, 1979, by Horacio Valdez; Carretta de la Muerte, 1974, by José Benjamín López; Cristo, 1970, by José Benjamín López, Russian olive covered with tree wax, black walnut. Courtesy José Benjamín and Irene López. Photo: Mary Peck.

a narrative of tradition they have created.[1]

In the introduction to this book, I suggested that exhibiting is a central strategy for cultural and expressive autonomy among wood-carvers, although, ironically, this is also the dominant culture's chosen means of presentation. By using showcase environments to display themselves and their work, contemporary carvers meet Anglo tradition seekers—such as tourists and collectors—on equal ground. Santeros display wood carvings in a variety of ways. Luisito Luján and Marco and Patricia Oviedo, for example, arrange their beautiful santos in familiar and pleasing displays. Using the accoutrements of museums and galleries, such as directional signs, price lists, guest books, and business cards, they offer visitors access to their valuable artworks. In fact, the nature of the display can sometimes even increase carvings' costs, as in the Oviedos' distinction between high gallery prices for ready-made santos and lower studio prices for commissions.

Artists and others also use exhibition techniques for creating displays for themselves and their families and friends. José Benjamín López and Enrique Rendón's sister, Dulcinea López, have created religious altars from their handmade santos. José Benjamín López's home altar, arranged dramatically in a dark alcove of his living room and including a life-size image of a bloody Christ, a Mexican carving of the Madonna, three santos on a tiered platform, a large carretta, and an elongated unpainted Cristo, with candles placed in front of many of the objects, has a staged quality similar to Oviedo's adobe art gallery. But it is also an older, more intimate mode of presentation, not as tourist-friendly as Oviedo's. The pieces are serious, religious, and artful. The display is purposeful. Although, increasingly, López welcomes potential art patrons to his house, his altar is arranged for his family and his wood-carving friends, not necessarily for the recreational traveler. Within the framework of the politics of ethnic identity, López's altar combines museum techniques with a more personal, religious expression. Some critics question whether minority cultures can appropriate the dominant culture's strategies and still achieve independent expressive voices. They fear appropriation is dangerous, possibly a strategy for absorbing rejection more than a genuine means of cultural expression.[2] However, at least for contemporary New Mexican santeros, exhibiting, with its corollaries, marketing and museumizing, are as much a part of crafting tradition as religion and spirituality.

But santo production flourishes in New Mexico for reasons other than the carvers' appropriation of elite display techniques. One could even argue that santos thrive in spite of the carvers' displays. Contemporary santeros call on a variety of resources. Patricia Oviedo collects *Far Side* comics, one of which provided her joke about finding cowasaurus rexes and bovidactyls on our burro ride, in the same spirit of delight and mild opposition that she brings to all aspects of her family's donkey and santo-making enterprise. Enrique Rendón referred to Marvel comics and children's picture books of saints to produce handmade santos for a discerning clientele seeking cultural authenticity. Although less self-consciously than Oviedo, Rendón used resources from popular culture, although they had little to do with his patrons' expectations.

Just as patrons look to santos as symbols of tradition, contemporary santeros single out certain wood-carvers to discover tradition's meaning. Specifically, contemporary carvers pay special homage to Patrocinio Barela and Enrique Rendón. Barela and Rendón were deeply religious and passionately engaged in their wood carving, but both were iconoclasts. For a variety of reasons, including alcoholism and his refusal to conform to mid-twentieth-century assimilationist pressures, Barela was rejected by the Taos Hispano community. Rendón, who looked askance at the Anglo marketing policies other santeros embraced, rejected the commercial community. Neither Barela nor Rendón sought social or artistic alignments. Both practiced wood carving without attempting to define it. Even more than Barela, Rendón refused a romantic image. The two produced carvings for sale and to some extent allowed market demands to influence their styles, but they left the categorizing of their work to others. They crafted holy images and abstracts; they became emblematic for others who today craft tradition.

Like collectors and museum professionals, contemporary santeros have met the challenge of defining Barela's and Rendón's work. For them Barela's abstract carving is a type of cultural daring and Rendón's "cosmic" santos are true folk art. The contemporary carvers' appreciation of these artists is political more than aesthetic. It is determined by a need for ethnic self-awareness. For contemporary carvers, Barela and Rendón represent authenticity as much as any Spanish colonial image does. For today's carvers, Barela and Rendón represent liberation, freedom, and power.

Ironically, however, when carvers attempt to replicate the cultural daring of Barela in their own works, they reproduce the forms preferred by the elite fine-art world. Although early-twentieth-century modernists collected and exhibited Barela's work, they did not necessarily recognize his carvings as fine art, only as "second bests" to recognized masterpieces.[3] Thus, when contemporary carvers align themselves with Barela, Picasso, and modernism, they replicate a patronizing association that will ultimately not allow them full acceptance among cultural elites. They vie for artistic legitimacy on another culture's terms. Luis Tapia experiences this directly. His gallery has no place for his unpainted figurative and abstract sculpture.

Many might look to religion for cultural authenticity in santos, but there the market, the art world, and politics are linked. Historic churches place Spanish colonial and contemporary santos behind glass in much the same way that museums display them. When contemporary carvers, such as Luis Tapia or Marco and Patricia Oviedo, donate their artworks to churches, they assign a religious value to their art that has as much to do with ethnic identity, cultural ownership, and artistic patrimony as it does with filling a functional need of the parish. Placing contemporary santos in churches signifies a value for the pieces other than one derived from the marketplace. But it also often underscores the meaning of the church as a historic and cultural landmark.

Some carvings exist on a vernacular level, alongside of, but separate from, the prevailing Western art-culture system. For example, Rendón's image of San Antonio, placed by a local parishioner in La Capilla del Santo Niño in Chimayó, is indistinguishable from the plaster images next to it. Although tourists flock to this private chapel in El Potrero Plaza, the devotional displays inside are arranged by and for parishioners, not tourists. The Cristo that Horacio Valdez donated to the Lyden chapter of the Brotherhood of Our Father Jesus is practically invisible inside the morada, a place essentially closed to tourists and other outsiders. The Cristo has no place in the morada as art or commodity. Although both Rendón and Valdez made their santos to sell, their deep participation in religion was shared by other Hispano community members who used the artists' santos in devotion.

Inasmuch as all contemporary carvers mediate between the worlds of

Fig. 127. *Chima Altar Ford 3* (Chimayó
Dashboard Altar), 1991, by Luis Tapia, 48" x 60"
x 9". Collection: The Albuquerque Museum.
Photo: Craig Smith.

commerce and spirituality, many also deal with the two northern villages of Chimayó and Córdova, heavily visited by tourists since early in this century. Some carvers live in these villages, others come from elsewhere to sell their wood carvings in them, and still others recall these places in their art, as in Luis Tapia's recent *Chima Altar* (Chimayó Dashboard Altar), a conceptual altar about Chimayó Hispano culture, consisting of cars, religious imagery, and the desert landscape. As they do with tourists, individual carvers confront Chimayó and Córdova differently. Marco Oviedo, who lives in Chimayó, caters to outside visitors. Enrique Rendón, whose santos were commissioned by the Potrero Trading Post and are currently displayed in both churches of El Potrero Plaza, came from Velarde and had no experience with Chimayó's tradition of culture display. Unlike Oviedo, who uses Chimayó to construct and sell tradition to outsiders, Rendón arrived in Chimayó to show and sell his wood carvings to local vendors. Rendón participated in, rather than appropriated, Chimayó's tradition of culture display.

Crafting and selling tradition includes, but is not necessarily the same as, crafting and selling saints. Crafters and sellers of tradition, those who package an idea of cultural authenticity, are not necessarily those who actually produce saints. Sometimes tradition crafters, like most members of the Spanish Colonial Arts Society, are not even Hispano. Others, such as Escuela Artesana carvers, are Hispano artists who make abstracts along with saints. These abstracts, produced in the spirit of ethnic and artistic liberation, represent a reinvented tradition that stands apart from santos. Because of their opaque meaning and unconventional style as local art, abstracts are difficult to sell. On the other hand, Escuela Artesana carvers' santos, produced with the same devotion to cultural authenticity as abstracts, are more accessible to patrons and easier to sell. They are one component of a larger repertoire of crafting and selling tradition.

No matter whether they are illiterate or hold advanced degrees, santeros rely on books for making santos. They use them in a variety of ways. José Benjamín López reads art books about Picasso, Michelangelo, and other master Western artists. Enrique Rendón looked at children's books and comics for models for his saints. Marco Oviedo uses exhibition catalogues both for copying Spanish colonial santos and for legitimizing the authenticity of his craft. He also has the old book, about anatomy and making dyes, handed down in his family, a text that acts like some people's notions of handed-down tradition. For santeros, books have power.

Contemporary santos take many forms, including the varied polychrome styles of individual santeros, unpainted chip-carved images, abstracts like Barela's that have narrative content, and secular, or non-Catholic, images. Noah's Ark, an image taken from the Old Testament, is particularly popular. Carvers of the tale of the flood, such as Luis Tapia and Marco Oviedo, expand their santo repertoire to meet the demands of non-Catholic, mostly Jewish, patrons. It is reasonable to consider Old Testament santos as part of the commercial and aesthetic syncretism that occurs in contemporary New Mexico santo making. Whereas, for example, Luis Tapia and Enrique Rendón each produced images of Kateri Tekakwitha because of either economic or personal associations with Indians, Oviedo and Tapia make Noah's Arks to oblige an increasingly diversified clientele.

Contemporary santeros have many constituencies, and individual carvers interact with various groups and people differently. Their alliances are complex, running across cultural and political distinctions. For example, Enrique

Fig. 128. Bulto of San Martín de Porres, 1982, by Luisito Luján, cedar. Collection: Gene Autry Western Heritage Museum. Photo: Susan Einstein.

Rendón drew his inspiration from everyday experiences and associations. Feeling no need to define his political, commercial, or artistic goals, he allied himself with neither the nonconformist Escuela Artesana, nor the more mainstream Spanish Market. At different points in his career, Luis Tapia both organized young, Hispano activist artists from northern New Mexico villages and demonstrated wood carving to wealthy urban shoppers in a New York City department store. Marco Oviedo relies on the museumizing of Chimayó but has rejected the marketing practices of his uncle Jacobo Trujillo and artists from Córdova, who have sold carvings by craftspeople other than themselves in their shops. Oviedo prefers an exclusive clientele.

Although the markets, villages, galleries, and museums of New Mexico are mapped out for tourists, they are also available to santeros, as resources for crafting tradition and making and selling saints. Local culture displays in Chimayó include religious pilgrimages and lowriding as much as they do the Oviedos' burro rides, the Ortegas' and Trujillos' weavings, and enchiladas and sopaipillas at Rancho de Chimayó Restaurant. Everyday life occurs in this village, intertwined with the life of tourism. Although crafted by an Anglo board, Spanish Market offers Hispano craftspeople a semiannual reunion, and even artists who choose not to participate attend just to visit with peers and friends. Santa Fe galleries and museums hire local artists such as Luis Tapia to restore Spanish colonial art and furnishings. Many carvers credit the knowledge they have of eighteenth- and nineteenth-century santos to their examinations of museum collections. Along with the culture of tourism at these sites there is a culture of the subjects of tourism, the santeros. Santeros have their own motivations and influences that are separate from consumer culture; at the same time, they participate in that consumer culture.

Some santeros, such as Marco and Patricia Oviedo, are precisely in the business of tourism, of constructing a notion of cultural authenticity that fits their and their patrons' expectations but that also capitalizes on the couple's particular skills. Other carvers, such as Luis Tapia, José Benjamín López, and Luisito Luján, also search for authenticity in their wood carving, but the tradition they craft is based more on ideas about art and ethnic politics shared among local carvers than on individual, commercial enterprise. Thus they have the challenge of reconciling oppositional politics with modes of commerce sometimes beyond their control. A few, such as Enrique Rendón and Patrocinio Barela, allowed others to worry about notions of cultural authenticity while they produced and sold their unusual carvings. Other carvers who, like Rendón, are also *hermanos,* such as Charles Carrillo and Nicolás Herrera, negotiate the demands of their Spanish Market patrons with the spiritual value they attach to their work. In making life-sized carvings similar to those used by brothers in Holy Week processions, Herrerra brings his religion to the marketplace and to his restored adobe home in El Rito, where he holds annual exhibitions.

Although carvers work primarily within one or two of the frameworks of ethnic politics, fine art, tourism, or religion, their activities reflect a great mixture of these influences. The culture of the contemporary santero is dynamic, complex, and, often, reflexive. Carvers participate in the many worlds in which their santos appear, and they make choices about the meanings of their works. Although the dominant culture, including both the fine-art world and tourism, remains powerful among contemporary santeros, it also belongs to the carvers, to an extent. The market and, increasingly, the art world, are as much a part of

Fig. 129. Bulto of Nuestra Señora de los Dolores, 1990, by Gloria López Córdova. cedar, cottonwood. Collection: Gene Autry Western Heritage Museum. Photo: Susan Einstein.

the santo tradition as religion. So is the notion of tradition itself. Santeros constantly renegotiate ideas of the past and the present. Art world recognition, ethnic awareness, education, and commercial success, combined with religion, enhance the complexity of crafting their devotions and the making and selling of santos. In the late twentieth century, the mix of these influences strengthens the power of the saints and their makers, while illustrating their authenticity.

Fig. 130. Life-sized Cristo, 1992, by Nicolás Herrera, displayed in his restored adobe home, El Rito. Collection of the artist. Photo: Mary Peck.

NOTES

In citing works in the notes, short titles have generally been used. Works frequently cited have been identified by the following abbreviations:

EC   Ivan Karp and Steven D. Lavine, eds., *Exhibiting Cultures. The Poetics and Politics of Museum Display* (Washington, D.C.: Smithsonian Institution Press, 1991).

NPR   Lynn Kienholz and Ira Gusalimian, Audiotape of interview by Lynn Kienholz and Ira Gusalimian with Luis Tapia, Félix López, and Laurie Beth Kalb, during exhibition, "Santos, Statues and Sculpture," at Craft & Folk Art Museum, Los Angeles (Los Angeles: KCRW 89.9 FM, National Public Radio, Arts L.A., 25 July 1988).

WC   Charles L. Briggs, *The Woodcarvers of Córdova, New Mexico. Social Dimensions of an Artistic "Revival"* (Knoxville: University of Tennessee Press, 1980; paperback reprint, Albuquerque: University of New Mexico Press, 1989).

        Personal interviews provide the majority of data for this book. At the beginning of each chapter's notes, I list all conversations reflected by quotes and retellings in the text.

INTRODUCTION

1. Henry Glassie, *Turkish Traditional Art Today* (Bloomington: Indiana University Press, 1993), 473.
2. See Richard Handler, *Nationalism and the Politics of Culture in Quebec* (Madison: University of Wisconsin Press, 1988); Richard Handler and Jocelyn Linnekin, "Tradition, Genuine or Spurious," *Journal of American Folklore* 97, no. 385 (1984): 273–90; Charles L. Briggs, "On the Production of Scholarly Authority in Research on the 'Invention of Tradition'" (unpublished MS, 1993); John D. Dorst, *The Written Suburb. An American Site, An Ethnographic Dilemma* (Philadelphia: University of Pennsylvania Press, 1989), 132–33.

3. Charles L. Briggs, "To Talk in Different Tongues: The 'Discovery' and 'Encouragement' of Hispano Woodcarvers by Santa Fe Patrons, 1919–1945," in *Hispanic Crafts of the Southwest*, edited by William Wroth (Colorado Springs: Taylor Museum of the Colorado Springs Fine Arts Center, 1977), 37–52; idem, WC; idem, "The Role of *Mexicano* Artists and the Anglo Elite in the Emergence of a Contemporary Folk Art," in *Folk Art and Art Worlds*, eds. John Michael Vlach and Simon Bronner (Ann Arbor: UMI Research Press, 1986), 195–224.

4. Suzanne Forrest, *The Preservation of the Village. New Mexico's Hispanics and the New Deal* (Albuquerque: University of New Mexico Press, 1989), 53–54; William Wroth, *Furniture from the Hispanic Southwest* (Santa Fe: Ancient City Press, 1984), v.

5. Thomas J. Steele, S. J., *Santos and Saints: The Religious Folk Art of Hispanic New Mexico* (Albuquerque: Calvin Horn, 1974; Santa Fe: Ancient City Press, 1982), 174–79.

6. George Mills, *The People of the Saints* (Colorado Springs: Taylor Museum of the Colorado Springs Fine Arts Center, 1967), 7–8.

7. James Clifford, "On Collecting Art and Culture," in *The Predicament of Culture. Twentieth-Century Ethnography, Literature, and Art*, ed. James Clifford (Cambridge: Harvard University Press, 1988), 215–51; Sally Price, *Primitive Art in Civilized Places* (Chicago: University of Chicago Press, 1989).

8. William Wroth, *Christian Images in Hispanic New Mexico* (Colorado Springs: Taylor Museum of the Colorado Springs Fine Arts Center, 1982), ix.

9. See Price, *Primitive Art*, 1.

10. Dorst, *Written Suburb*, 127–29.

11. Barbara Kirshenblatt-Gimblett, pers. com., 1992.

12. Barbara Kirshenblatt-Gimblett, "Objects of Ethnography," EC, 419.

13. Marianne L. Stoller, "'Peregrinas' with Many Visions," in *The Desert is No Lady. Southwestern Landscapes in Women's Writing and Art*, ed. Vera Norwood and Janice Monk (New Haven: Yale University Press, 1987), 132.

1. CHICANO ART AND SANTOS

Interviews: Anonymous, 3 August 1990; Charles M. Carrillo, 2 August 1990, 4 October 1990; Félix López, 31 July 1990; Wilberto Miera, February 1988, 10 October 1990; Nat Owings, 28 July 1990; Luis Tapia, 2 August 1984, February 1988, 1 February 1990, 7 September 1990, September 1990.

1. Tomás Ybarra-Frausto, "*The Chicano Movement/The Movement of Chicano Art,*" in EC, 128–50.

2. NPR.

3. WC, 210.

4. Anne Hillerman, "The New Santeros," in *Santa Fe New Mexican* 23 October 1977, 5.

5. E. Boyd, *Popular Arts of Spanish New Mexico* (Santa Fe: Museum of New Mexico Press, 1974).

6. Marianne L. Stoller in William Wroth, *Hispanic Crafts of the Southwest* (Colorado Springs: Taylor Museum of the Colorado Springs Fine Arts Center, 1977), 88–89; Wroth, *Hispanic Crafts of the Southwest*, 113.

7. Hillerman, "*New Santeros*," 5.

8. Ybarra-Frausto, "*Chicano Movement*," 136.

9. La Cofradía de Artes y Artesanos Hispanicos. By-Laws (Santa Fe: N.p., n.d.).

10. See Ybarra-Frausto, "Chicano Movement," 131.

11. Paul Sturiale, "Artists Work to Save Heritage," in *Santa Fe New Mexican*, [1978].

12. WC, 52; Ann Vedder, "History of Spanish Colonial Arts Society, Inc., 1951–1981," in *Hispanic Arts and Ethnohistory in the Southwest. New Papers Inspired by the Work of E. Boyd*, ed. Marta Weigle with Claudia Larcombe and Samuel Larcombe (Santa Fe: Ancient City Press, 1983), 211.

13. WC, 50–53.

14. NPR.

15. *Chispas! Cultural Warriors of New Mexico* (Phoenix: Heard Museum, 1992), 28.

16. Lonn Taylor and Dessa Bokides, *New Mexican Furniture, 1600–1940. The Origins, Survival, and Revival of Furniture Making in the Hispanic Southwest* (Santa Fe: Museum of New Mexico Press, 1987).

17. See Ybarra-Frausto, "Chicano Movement, 147.

18. See Taylor and Bokides, *New Mexican Furniture, 1600–1940,* 1987.

19. NPR.

20. Ibid.

21. Clifford, *Predicament of Culture,* 92–97, 215–51.

22. NPR.

23. Taylor and Bokides, *New Mexican Furniture, 1600–1940,* 218; George Kubler, *The Religious Architecture of New Mexico. In the Colonial Period and Since the American Occupation* (Colorado Springs: Taylor Museum of the Colorado Springs Fine Arts Center, 1940; Albuquerque: University of New Mexico Press for the School of American Research, 1972), 142.

24. Kubler, *Religious Architecture of New Mexico,* 65; Boyd, *Popular Arts,* 353.

25. Boyd, *Popular Arts,* 353. Churches with carvings of the Christ of Esquipulas by Molleno include the Santuario de Chimayó, the church of Cristo Rey in Santa Fe, designed by John Gaw Meem, the mission at Santa Clara Pueblo, and the chapel of St. Francis in Ranchos de Taos.

26. NPR.

27. Reverend Lawrence G. Lovasik, S. V. D., *New Picture Book of Saints: Illustrated Lives of the Saints for Young and Old* (1962; reprint, New York: Catholic Book Publishing, 1981).

28. NPR.

29. Ibid.

30. James Clifford, "Histories of the Tribal and the Modern," *Art in America* 73, no. 4 (1985): 171.

31. Boyd, *Popular Arts,* 167, 366–67.

32. Ybarra-Frausto, "Chicano Movement," 145.

33. *Sources and Inspirations: Paintings by Paul Pletka* (Santa Fe: Museum of Fine Arts, Museum of New Mexico, 1990), 11–41.

34. Carrillo in *Sources and Inspirations,* 29–33.

35. Ibid., 33.

36. NPR.

37. José E. Espinosa, *Saints in the Valleys. Christian Sacred Images in the History, Life and Folk Art of Spanish New Mexico* (Albuquerque: University of New Mexico Press, 1960; Albuquerque: University of New Mexico Press, 1967), ix; WC, 6.

38. WC, 193.

39. NPR.

40. Robert Goldwater, *Primitivism in Modern Art* (New York: Random House, 1938; enl. ed., Cambridge: Harvard University Press, Belknap Press, 1986), 233–35, 243–46.

41. Ibid., 234, 244.

42. Boyd, *Popular Arts,* 369–71.

43. John J. Bodine, "A Tri-Ethnic Trap: The Spanish-Americans in Taos," in *Spanish-Speaking People in the United States. Proceedings of the 1968 Annual Spring Meeting of the American Ethnological Society,* ed. June Helm (Seattle: University of Washington Press, 1968), 149; Sylvia Rodríguez, "Land, Water, and Ethnic Identity in Taos," in *Land, Water, and Culture. New Perspectives on Hispanic Land Grants,* ed. Charles L. Briggs and John R. Van Ness (Albuquerque: University of New Mexico Press, 1987), 345.

44. Ybarra-Frausto, "Chicano Movement," 146.

2. Primitivism, Modernism, and Patrocinio Barela

Interviews: Anonymous, August 1990, 2 November 1990, 26 November 1990; Luis Barela, Sr., 11 December 1990; Dr. J. A. Domínguez, 3 August 1990; Ted Egri and Kit Egri, 11 December 1990; Woolcott Ely, 11 December 1990; Félix López, 22 June 1984; José Benjamín López, 1990; Thomas Merlan, 14 August 1984, 2 August 1990; Ben Tafoya, 23 September 1991; Luis Tapia, 26 July 1989, 1990; David Witt, 10 May 1989.

1. Henry Glassie, "Folk Art," in *Folklore and Folklife. An Introduction,* ed. Richard M. Dorson (Chicago: University of Chicago Press, 1972), 272; Franz Boas, *Primitive Art* (Oslo: H. Aschehough, 1927; paperback reprint, New York: Dover Publications, 1955), 40–54.

2. See Boas, *Primitive Art,* 69–80.

3. Barela said he was born in 1908. Taos Harwood Foundation curator David Witt places his birth as early as 1900.

4. Mildred Crews, Wendell Anderson, and Judson Crews, *Patrocinio Barela: Taos Woodcarver* (1955; reprint, Taos, N.M.: Taos Recordings and Publications, 1976), 5.

5. David Witt, pers. com.; José Benjamín López, "A Perspective on the Work of Patrocinio Barela" (unpublished MS, 1980); idem, "Patrocinio Barela" (unpublished MS, 1980).

6. Crews, Anderson, and Crews, *Patrocinio Barela.*

7. *Taos News,* 29 October 1964.

8. Ted Egri, pers. com.; Woolcott Ely, pers. com.; Holger Cahill, Papers, WPA file (Archives of American Art, Smithsonian Institution, Washington, D.C., n.d.).

9. *Taos News,* 29 October 1964.

10. Bodine, "A Tri-Ethnic Trap," 146.

11. Rodríguez, "Land, Water, and Ethnic Identity," 345; Bodine, "A Tri-Ethnic Trap," 147.

12. Ben Tafoya, pers. com.; Rodríguez, "Land, Water, and Ethnic Identity," 348.

13. William Clark, "Working with the Grain. Félix López: A Response to Religion. Luis Barela: A Response to the Wood," in *Albuquerque Journal,* 27 July 1990, C13.

14. Cahill, Papers, WPA file, 2; Phaedra Greenwood, "The Mother, the Struggle, the Search, the Heart. The Story of Patrocinio Barela" *New Mexico Craft* 3, no. 1 (1980): 14.

15. Cahill, Papers, WPA file, 2, 3; Greenwood, "The Mother, the Struggle," 15.

16. Cahill, Papers, WPA file, 2.

17. Edward W. Said, *Orientalism* (New York: Vintage Books, 1978), 1.

18. Van Deren Coke, *Taos and Santa Fe: The Artist's Environment* (Albuquerque: University of New Mexico Press, published for the Amon Carter Museum of Western Art, Ft. Worth, Texas, and the Art Gallery, University of New Mexico, 1963), 12.

19. Said, *Orientalism,* 3, 5.

20. Julie Schimmel, "From Salon to Pueblo: The First Generation," in *Art in New Mexico, 1900–1945. Paths to Taos and Santa Fe* (Washington, D.C.: National Museum of American Art and Abbeville Press, 1986), 48–49; Sharyn R. Udall, *Modernist Painting in New Mexico 1913–1935* (Albuquerque: University of New Mexico Press, 1984), 172, 205.

21. Keith L. Bryant, "The Atchison, Topeka and Santa Fe Railway and the Development of the Taos and Santa Fe Art Colonies" *Western Historical Quarterly* 9, no. 4 (1978): 451–52; Marta Weigle and Kyle Fiore, *Santa Fe and Taos: The Writer's Era, 1916–1941* (Santa Fe: Ancient City Press, 1982), 27–29; Marta Weigle, "Dancer, Pilgrim, Trader and Tourist in the Development of a Southwestern Folklore" (unpublished MS, 1983), 23; Udall, *Modernist Painting,* 5.

22. Sarah J. Nestor, *The Native Market of the Spanish New Mexican Craftsmen in Santa Fe, 1933–1940* (Santa Fe: Colonial New Mexico Historical Foundation, 1978), 6–8, 11–18; Schimmel, "From Salon to Pueblo," 112; William Wroth, "New Hope in Hard Times: Hispanic Crafts are Revived During Troubled Years" *El Palacio* 89, no. 2 (1983): 22–31.

23. Udall, *Modernist Painting,* 5.

24. Briggs, "Role of Mexicano Artists," 216.

25. Crews, Anderson, and Crews, *Patrocinio Barela,* 8.

26. Patrocinio Barela, Papers (Taos, N.M.: Harwood Library Archives, n.d.).

27. Ted Egri to Laurie Beth Kalb, 4 August 1990; *Taos News,* 29 October 1964.

28. In his description of Barela's forgery, Manchester mentions that the process of "antiquing" has been practiced over a long period. It continues today. Woodcarver Wilberto Miera applies fertilizer to new wood to make, as he calls them, "instant antiques" (pers. com., February 1991). Santero Frank Brito, Sr. also antiques bultos, coating them with an egg mixture and baking them in an oven (pers. com.).

29. John Manchester, Papers (Taos, N.M.: Harwood Foundation Library), 16 November 78.

30. Price, *Primitive Art,* 115–16.

31. Anonymous, pers. com.. Barela was not the only woodcarver who cursed his work. See page 169 for a discussion of Córdovan woodcarver José Dolores López's use of monos for santos.

32. Merlan, pers. com.; Woolcott Ely, pers. com..

33. Honorary pallbearers included Craig Vincent, Richard Daley, Manuel Berg, Dr. J. A. Domínguez, Richard Dicus, Martin Vargas, Ted Egri, Harold Street, Judson Crews, Wendell Anderson, Clark Funk, and Lozier Funk (*Taos News,* 29 October 1964).

34. Russell Vernon Hunter, "*Anatomy of God,*" in Russell Vernon Hunter Papers, Archives of American Art, Smithsonian Institution, [1942].

35. WC, 86; Crews, Anderson, and Crews, *Patrocinio Barela,* 9.

36. Virginia Hunter Ewing, "Some Memories Concerning New Mexico's WPA-Federal Art Project" (unpublished MS, 1988), 6.

37. Russell Vernon Hunter, Papers.

38. E. Boyd, Federal Art Project Memoirs, Archives of American Art, 1936–37.

39. *El Independiente,* 23 August 1974.

40. Russell Vernon Hunter, "Concerning Patrocinio Barela," in *Art for the Millions. Essays from the 1930s by Artists and Administrators of the WPA Federal Art Project,* ed. Francis V. O'Connor and with an Introduction (1937; reprint, Boston: New York Graphic Society, 1975), 99.

41. José Griego y Maestas, "A New Generation of Santeros" *New Mexico Magazine* 60, no. 8 (1982): 24–31. The core membership consists of José Benjamín López, his brother Leroy López, Félix López, his brother Manuel López, Olivar Martínez, Clyde Salazar, Olivar Rivera, José Griego y Maestas, and Luisito Luján.

42. Félix López, pers. com.; Clark, "Working with the Grain," C14.

43. See Louise Cox and Ray Telles, Santeros, 16 mm and 1/2" video, 28 min. (Distributed by Tapestry International, New York and Indiana University Audio-Visual Center, Bloomington, Indiana, 1986).

44. Ibid.

45. López, "Patrocinio Barela," 3.

46. López, "Patrocinio Barela"; idem, "A Perspective on the Work of Patrocinio Barela," 14.

47. Clark, "Working with the Grain," C13.

48. See Rodríguez, "Land, Water, and Ethnic Identity."

49. Dorst, *Written Suburb,* 131–35.

50. See Liza Kurwin and Andrew Connors, Videotaped interview with Leo Salazar, National Museum of American Art, Smithsonian Institution, 1987.

51. Ibid.

3. Spanish Colonial Replicas by Oviedo Carvings and Bronze

Interviews: Anonymous, pers. com.; Zoraida Ortega, n.d.; Jacobo Javier, (J. J.), Oviedo, 13 April 1991; Marco A. Oviedo, 7 May 1988, 9 April 1991, 10 April 1991; Patricia Trujillo Oviedo, 10 April 1991, July 1991.

1. WC, 3.

2. Kirshenblatt-Gimblett, "Objects of Ethnography," 413.

3. See Clifford, *Predicament of Culture;* Dorst, *Written Suburb;* and EC for discussions of the way museums and some local communities fragment culture in their displays.

4. Bill Field, a board member and past president of the Spanish Colonial Arts Society, is the son of Lois Field, an early supporter, in the 1950s, of the Society's revitalization (Vedder 1983:206, 210, 212). Bud Redding is the current Spanish Colonial Arts Society Director.

5. *WPA Guide to 1930s New Mexico,* originally published as *New Mexico. A Guide to the Colorful State* (New York: Hastings House, 1940; Tucson: University of Arizona Press, 1989), 298; Forrest, *Preservation of the Village,* 151; Ward Alan Minge, *"Efectos del Pais:* A History of Weaving Along the Rio Grande," in *Spanish Textile Tradition of New Mexico and Colorado,* ed. Nora Fisher (Santa Fe: Museum of New Mexico Press, 1979), 21–22.

6. Suzanne Baizerman, "Textiles, Traditions and Tourist Art: Hispanic Weaving in Northern New Mexico," Ph. D. dissertation, University of Minnesota, 1987.

7. I follow the discussion of shaping the past in Dorst, *Written Suburb,* 198.

8. See WC.

9. Marta Weigle, "The First Twenty-Five Years of the Spanish Colonial Arts Society," in *Hispanic Arts and Ethnohistory in the Southwest,* ed. Marta Weigle with Claudia Larcombe and Samuel Larcombe (Santa Fe: Ancient City Press, 1983), 185.

10. Elizabeth Althea Kay, *Chimayó Valley Traditions* (Santa Fe: Ancient City Press, 1987), 3.

11. Kirshenblatt-Gimblett, "Objects of Ethnography," 407.

12. See James Clifford, "Four Northwest Coast Museums: Travel Reflections," in EC, 240, for comparative observations of tribal museum displays.

13. See Dean MacCannell, *The Tourist. A New Theory of the Leisure Class* (New York: Schocken Books, 1976; New York: Schocken Books, 1989), 109–33.

14. See David Lowenthal, "Age and Artifact. Dilemmas of Appreciation," in *The Interpretation of Ordinary Landscapes. Geographical Essays,* ed. D. W. Meinig (New York: Oxford University Press, 1979), 113.

15. Patricia Oviedo in Jim Sagel, "Burro Ride Offers View, 300 Years of History," in *Journal North,* 4 July 1984, E-4.

16. Kirshenblatt-Gimblett, "Objects of Ethnography," 419.

17. Charles L. Briggs, "The Carved Animals of New Mexico. Chicano Art and the World of 'Folk Art'" (unpublished MS, 1985), 1.

18. See Lowenthal, "Age and Artifact," 124.

19. Umberto Eco, *Travels in Hyper Reality: Essays* (San Diego: Harcourt Brace Jovanovich, 1986), 1–58.

20. See Barbara Kirshenblatt-Gimblett, "Authenticity and Authority in the Representation of Culture: The Poetics and Politics of Tourist Production," in "Kulturkontakt/Kulturkonflikt: Zur Erfahrung des Fremden," ed. Ina Maria Greverus, Konrad Kostlin, and Heinz Schilling, *Notizen* 28, no. 1 (1988): 60–61.

21. *The Wingspread Collector's Guide: Santa Fe and Taos* (Albuquerque: Wingspread Communications, 1988).

22. Marco A. Oviedo, pers. com.; *The Wingspread Collector's Guide,* 1988.

23. Ibid.

24. Zoraidia Ortega, pers. com.; Marianne L. Stoller, "'Peregrinas' with Many Visions," 134.

25. Mills, *People of the Saints.*

26. Marco A. Oviedo, pers. com.; See Laurie Beth Kalb, *Santos, Statues and Sculpture: Contemporary Woodcarving in New Mexico* (Los Angeles: Craft & Folk Art Museum, 1988), 18.

27. Wroth, *Christian Images,* 167–68, pl. 13.

28. MacCannell, *Tourist,* 387–88.

29. Daniel Boorstin in MacCannell, *Tourist,* 103.

30. See MacCannell, *Tourist,* 105–7.

31. *The Wingspread Collector's Guide: Santa Fe and Taos* (Albuquerque: Wingspread Incorporated, 1991), vol. 5, no. 1.

32. *Wingspread Collector's Guide,* 1991.

33. See Deirdre Evans-Pritchard, "How 'They' See 'Us.' Native American Images of Tourists," in *Annals of Tourism Research* 16, no. 1 (1989): 91.

34. William Clements in Evans-Pritchard, "How 'They' See 'Us,'" 93; see also William Clements, "The Ethnic Joke as Mirror Culture" *New York Folklore* 12, no. 3–4 (1986): 95.

35. Evans-Pritchard, "How 'They' See 'Us,'" 94, 96.

36. Clifford Geertz 1986:380; Kirshenblatt-Gimblett, "Authenticity and Authority," 62.

37. Kirshenblatt-Gimblett, "Authenticity and Authority," 61–62.

38. See Edward Bruner and Phyllis Gorfain, "Dialogic Narration and the Paradoxes of Masada," in *Text, Play and Story: The Construction and Reconstruction of Self and Society,* ed. Edward M. Bruner, Proceedings of the American Ethnological Society (Washington, D.C.: American Ethnological Society, 1984), 73.

4. ENRIQUE RENDÓN: A FOLK ARTIST'S FOLK ARTIST

Interviews: Anonymous, 31 July 1991; Elma Bal, July 1984, 21 August 1991; Dulcinea López, Spring 1991; Joe López, 13 July 1991; Eulogio Ortega, 12 July 1984, 26 September 1991; Zoraida Ortega, 29 July 1991; Enrique Rendón, summer 1983, summer 1984, 12 July 1984, 25 July 1984; Raymond Smith, 31 July 1991; Luis Tapia, n.d., 2 August 1984.

1. See Clifford, "On Collecting Art and Culture," 249–50.

2. See Dorst, *Written Suburb,* 200–201.

3. Marta Weigle, *Hispanic Villages of Northern New Mexico. A Reprint of Volume II of The 1935 Tewa Basin Study, with Supplementary Materials* (Santa Fe: Lightning Tree Press, 1975), 178–84.

4. T. M. Pearce, *New Mexico Place Names. A Geographical Dictionary* (Albuquerque: University of New Mexico Press, 1965; reprint, with corrections, Albuquerque: University of New Mexico Press, 1975), 103.

5. Chuck Rosenak, *Museum of American Folk Art Encyclopedia of Twentieth-Century American Folk Art and Artists* (New York: Abbeville Press, 1991), 256.

6. Eulogio Ortega to Laurie Beth Kalb, 6 August 1991.

7. Rosenak, *Museum of American Folk Art Encyclopedia,* 308–9; Jocelyn Lieu, "Prayers Help, Santero Says in Describing Craft," in *Rio Grande Sun,* 31 March 1983.

8. Eulogio Ortega to Laurie Beth Kalb, 6 August 1991.

9. Ibid.

10. See Bainbridge Bunting, *Taos Adobes: Spanish Colonial and Territorial Architecture in the Taos Valley* (Santa Fe: Museum of New Mexico Press, 1964), 4–5; idem, *Early Architecture in New Mexico* (Albuquerque: University of New Mexico Press, 1976), 63; Boyd, *Popular Arts,* 26.

11. See Dorst, *Written Suburb,* 199–200.

12. Eulogio Ortega to Laurie Beth Kalb, 6 August 1991.

13. Rosenak, *Museum of American Folk Art Encyclopedia,* 256.

14. Michael Owen Jones, *The Handmade Object and Its Maker* (Berkeley and Los Angeles: University of California Press, 1975; Lexington: University Press of Kentucky, 1989), 24.

15. Louis J. Chiaramonte, *Craftsman-Client Contracts: Interpersonal Relations in a Newfoundland Fishing Community* (St. John's, Newfoundland: Institute of Social and Economic Research, Memorial University of Newfoundland, 1970), 51.

16. Chiaramonte, *Craftsman-Client Contracts*, 51.

17. Donald Attwater, *The Avenel Dictionary of Saints*, published in 1979 as *The Penguin Dictionary of Saints* (New York: Penguin Books, 1965; New York: Avenel Books, 1981), 77–78; Steele, *Santos and Saints*, 182.

18. See WC.

19. Ibid., 47–50.

20. See Dorst, *Written Suburb*, 192–203.

21. Rosenak, *Museum of American Folk Art Encyclopedia*, 256.

22. Susan Stewart, *On Longing. Narratives of the Miniature the Gigantic, the Souvenir, the Collection* (Baltimore: Johns Hopkins University Press, 1984), 144–45.

23. See Nelson Graburn in Stewart, *On Longing*, 148; also Nelson H. H. Graburn, ed., *Ethnic and Tourist Arts: Cultural Expressions of the Fourth World* (Berkeley and Los Angeles: University of California Press, 1979), 2–3.

24. WC, 6; Espinosa, *Saints in the Valleys*, ix.

25. WC, 192–93.

26. Wroth, *Christian Images*, 206.

27. Glassie, "Folk Art," 253–81.

28. Eulogio Ortega to Laurie Beth Kalb, 6 August 1991.

29. See Espinosa, *Saints in the Valleys*, 51; Steele, *Santos and Saints*, 1–27.

30. Boyd, *Popular Arts*, 145–49; WC, 11.; Espinosa, *Saints in the Valleys*, 52.

31. Yvonne Lange, "Lithography, an Agent of Technological Change in Religious Folk Art: A Thesis" *Western Folklore* 33, no. 1 (1974): 56–57.

32. Dextra Frankel, Thomas Mercer Hartman, and the Albuquerque Museum, *One Space/Three Visions* (Albuquerque: Albuquerque Museum, 1979), 195–68.

33. See Alfred Metraux, *Voodoo in Haiti*, trans. Hugo Charteris (1959; reprint, with new introduction by Sidney W. Mintz, New York: Schocken Books, 1972), 23–358, for a discussion of cultural syncretism.

34. Attwater, *Avenel Dictionary of Saints*, 234–35.

35. Ibid., 235.

36. Eulogio Ortega to Laurie Beth Kalb, 6 August 1991.

37. Marta Weigle, *Brothers of Light, Brothers of Blood. The Penitentes of the Southwest* (Santa Fe: Ancient City Press, 1976), 146–47.

38. Eulogio Ortega to Laurie Beth Kalb, 6 August 1991.

39. See E. Boyd, *The New Mexico Santero* (Santa Fe: Museum of New Mexico Press, 1969), 17.

40. Kalb, *Santos, Statues and Sculpture*.

41. The brotherhood practice of Las Tinieblas resembles the Tenebrae services of the Roman Catholic church. It is that portion of the Holy Week ceremonies that commemorates the three hours of darkness that fell over the earth just before Christ died (Weigle 1976:174–75).

42. WC, 12.

43. I borrow the term myth of tradition from Dorst, *Written Suburb*, 127–29.

5. Crafting Devotions, Crafting Tradition

1. I borrow the term *traditioning* from Dorst, *Written Suburb*, 133.

2. Lowery Stokes Sims in Lucy R. Lippard, *Mixed Blessings. New Art in a Multicultural America* (New York: Pantheon Books, 1990), 233.

3. Price, *Primitive Art*, 96.

BIBLIOGRAPHY

Ahlborn, Richard E. "Spanish Colonial Wood Carving in New Mexico, 1590–1848." Master's thesis, University of Delaware, 1958.

———. "The Penitente Moradas of Abiquiu." *Contributions from the Museum of History and Technology,* Paper 63. Washington, D.C.: Smithsonian Institution Press, 1968. Reprint, with author's preface and two new photographs, Washington, D.C.: Smithsonian Institution Press, 1986.

Ahlborn, Richard E. and Harry R. Rubinstein. "Smithsonian Santos: Collecting and the Collection." In *Hispanic Arts and Ethnohistory in the Southwest,* edited by Marta Weigle with Claudia Larcombe and Samuel Larcombe, 241–83. Santa Fe: Ancient City Press, 1983.

Attwater, Donald. *The Avenel Dictionary of Saints.* Published in 1979 as *The Penguin Dictionary of Saints.* New York: Penguin Books, 1965; New York: Avenel Books, 1981.

Babcock, Barbara A. "Reflexivity: Definitions and Discriminations." *Semiotica* 30, no. 1/2 (1980): 1–14.

———. "Modeled Selves: Helen Cordero's 'Little People'." In *The Anthropology of Experience,* edited by Victor W. Turner and Edward M. Bruner, 316–44. Urbana: University of Illinois Press, 1986.

Babcock, Barbara A., Guy Monthan, and Doris Monthan. *The Pueblo Story-teller: Development of a Figurative Ceramic Tradition.* Tucson: University of Arizona Press, 1986.

Barela, Patrocinio. Papers. Harwood Foundation Library, Taos, N.M., n.d.

Bauman, Richard, and Roger D. Abrahams, eds. *"And Other Neighborly Names": Social Process and Cultural Image in Texas Folklore.* Austin: University of Texas Press, 1981.

Baizerman, Suzanne. "Textiles, Traditions and Tourist Art: Hispanic Weaving in Northern New Mexico." Ph.D. diss., University of Minnesota, 1987.

Beardsley, John, and Jane Livingston, eds. *Hispanic Art in the United States: Thirty Contemporary Painters and Sculptors.* Houston: Museum of Fine Arts and Abbeville Press, 1987.

Blumenschein, Ernest L. "Origin of the Taos Art Colony." *El Palacio* 20 (1926): 190–93.

Boas, Franz. *Primitive Art.* Oslo: H. Aschehough, 1927. Paperback reprint, New York: Dover Publications, 1955.

Bodine, John J. "A Tri-Ethnic Trap: The Spanish-Americans in Taos." In *Spanish-Speaking People in the United States: Proceedings of the 1968 Annual Spring Meeting of the American Ethnological Society,* edited by June Helm, 145–53. Seattle: University of Washington Press, 1968.

Boyd, E. Federal Art Project Memoirs, 1936–37. Archives of American Art,

Smithsonian Institution, Washington, D.C.

———. "Celso Gallegos—A Truly Spontaneous Primitive Artist." *El Palacio* 60, no. 5 (1953): 214–16.

———. *The New Mexico Santero.* Santa Fe: Museum of New Mexico Press, 1969.

———. *Popular Arts of Spanish New Mexico.* Santa Fe: Museum of New Mexico Press, 1974.

Briggs, Charles L. "To Talk in Different Tongues: The 'Discovery' and 'Encouragement' of Hispano Woodcarvers by Santa Fe Patrons, 1919–1945." In *Hispanic Crafts of the Southwest,* edited by William Wroth, 37–52. Colorado Springs: Taylor Museum of the Colorado Springs Fine Arts Center, 1977.

———. *The Woodcarvers of Córdova, New Mexico. Social Dimensions of an Artistic "Revival."* Knoxville: University of Tennessee Press, 1980. Paperback reprint, Albuquerque: University of New Mexico Press, 1989.

———. "The Carved Animals of New Mexico. Chicano Art and the World of 'Folk Art.'" Unpublished MS, 1985.

———. "The Role of *Mexicano* Artists and the Anglo Elite in the Emergence of a Contemporary Folk Art." In *Folk Art and Art Worlds,* edited by John Michael Vlach and Simon J. Bronner, 195–224. Ann Arbor: UMI Research Press, 1986.

———. *Competence in Performance. The Creativity of Tradition in Mexicano Verbal Art.* Philadelphia: University of Pennsylvania Press, 1988.

———. "On the Production of Scholarly Authority in Research on the 'Invention of Tradition.'" Unpublished MS, 1993.

Bright, Robert. *The Life and Death of Little Jo.* New York: Doubleday, Doran & Company, 1944.

Brody, J. J. "The Creative Consumer: Survival, Revival and Invention in Southwest Indian Arts." In *Ethnic and Tourist Arts: Cultural Expressions from the Fourth World,* edited by Nelson H. H. Graburn, 70–84. Berkeley and Los Angeles: University of California Press, 1976.

Brown, Lorin W., Charles L. Briggs, and Marta Weigle. *Hispano Folklife of New Mexico: The Lorin W. Brown Federal Writers' Project Manuscripts.* Albuquerque: University of New Mexico Press, 1978.

Bruner, Edward M., and Phyllis Gorfain. "Dialogic Narration and the Paradoxes of Masada." In *Text, Play and Story: The Construction and Reconstruction of Self and Society,* edited by Edward M. Bruner, 56–79. 1983 Proceedings of the American Ethnological Society. Washington, D.C.: American Ethnological Society, 1984.

Bruner, Edward M., ed. *Text, Play, and Story: The Construction and Reconstruction of Self and Society.* 1983 Proceedings of the American Ethnological Society. Washington, D.C.: American Ethnological Society, 1984.

Bryant, Keith L., Jr. "The Atchison, Topeka and Santa Fe Railway and the Development of the Taos and Santa Fe Art Colonies." *Western Historical Quarterly* 9, no. 4 (1978): 437–53.

Bullock, Alice. *Mountain Villages.* 1973. Revised 2d ed., Santa Fe: Sunstone Press, 1981.

Bunting, Bainbridge. *Early Architecture in New Mexico.* Albuquerque: University of New Mexico Press, 1976.

Bunting, Bainbridge, Jean Lee Booth, and William R. Sims. *Taos Adobes: Spanish Colonial and Territorial Architecture of the Taos Valley.* Santa Fe: Museum of New Mexico Press, 1964.

Cabeza de Baca, Fabiola. *We Fed Them Cactus.* Albuquerque: University of New Mexico Press, 1954.

Cahill, Holger. Papers. WPA file. Archives of American Art, Smithsonian Institution, n.d.

———. "Introduction." In *New Horizons in American Art.* New York: Museum of Modern Art, 1936.

Cantwell, Robert. *Ethnomimesis. Folklife and the Representation of Culture.* Chapel Hill: University of North Carolina Press, 1993.

Cash, Marie Romero. "Santos of the Northern New Mexico Village Churches. A Documentation Project." *El Palacio* 95, no. 2 (1990): 24–29.

Cassidy, Ina Sizer. "Art and Artists of New Mexico: Woodcarver." *New Mexico. The State Magazine of National Interest* 14, no. 11 (1936): 25, 33.

Cather, Willa. *Death Comes for the Archbishop.* New York: Alfred A. Knopf, 1927; New York: Vintage Books, 1971.

Chiaramonte, Louis J. *Craftsman-Client Contracts: Interpersonal Relations in a Newfoundland Fishing Community.* St. John's, Newfoundland: Institute of Social and Economic Research, Memorial University of Newfoundland, 1970.

Chispas! Cultural Warriors of New Mexico. Phoenix: Heard Museum, 1992.

Clark, William. "Working with the Grain. Félix López: A Response to Religion. Luis Barela: A Response to the Wood." *Albuquerque Journal,* 27 July 1990, pp. C1, C13, C14.

Clements, William. "The Ethnic Joke as Mirror of Culture." *New York Folklore* 12, no. 3–4 (1986): 87–97.

Clifford, James. "Histories of the Tribal and the Modern." *Art in America* 73, no. 4 (1985): 164–215.

———. "Identity in Mashpee." In *The Predicament of Culture. Twentieth-Century Ethnography, Literature, and Art,* edited by James Clifford, 277–349. Cambridge: Harvard University Press, 1988.

———. "On Collecting Art and Culture."

In *The Predicament of Culture. Twentieth-Century Ethnography, Literature, and Art*, edited by James Clifford, 215–51. Cambridge: Harvard University Press, 1988.

    The Predicament of Culture. Twentieth-Century Ethnography, Literature and Art. Cambridge: Harvard University Press, 1988.

    "Four Northwest Coast Museums: Travel Reflections." In *Exhibiting Cultures: The Poetics and Politics of Museum Display,* edited by Ivan Karp and Steven D. Lavine, 212–54. Washington, D.C.: Smithsonian Institution Press, 1991.

Clifford, James, and George E. Marcus, eds. *Writing Culture. The Poetics and Politics of Ethnography.* A School of American Research Advanced Seminar. Berkeley and Los Angeles: University of California Press, 1986.

Cobos, Rubén. *A Dictionary of New Mexico and Southern Colorado Spanish.* Santa Fe: Museum of New Mexico Press, 1983.

Coe, Ralph T. *Lost and Found Traditions: Native American Art 1965–1985.* New York: American Federation of the Arts, 1986.

La Cofradía de Artes y Artesanos Hispanicos. By-Laws. Santa Fe, New Mexico, n.d..

Coke, Van Deren. *Taos and Santa Fe: The Artist's Environment, 1882–1942.* Albuquerque: University of New Mexico Press, 1963. Published for the Amon Carter Museum of Western Art, Ft. Worth, Texas and the Art Gallery, University of New Mexico.

    Andrew Dasburg. Albuquerque: University of New Mexico Press, 1979.

Córdova, Lorenzo de [Lorin W. Brown]. *Echoes of the Flute.* Santa Fe: Ancient City Press, 1972.

Cox, Louise, and Ray Telles. *Santeros.* 16 mm and 1/2" video, 28 min. Distributed by Tapestry International, New York and Indiana University Audio-Visual Center, Bloomington, Indiana, 1986.

Crews, Mildred T. "Patrocinio Barela: Woodcarver of Taos." *Presbyterian Life* 21, no. 4 (1968): 7–11.

Crews, Mildred, Wendell Anderson, and Judson Crews. *Patrocinio Barela: Taos Woodcarver.* 1955. Reprint, Taos, N.M.: Taos Recordings and Publications, 1976.

Dawson, Lawrence E., Vera-Mae Fredrickson, and Nelson H. H. Graburn, eds. *Traditions in Transition. Culture Contact and Material Change.* Berkeley and Los Angeles: Lowie Museum of Anthropology, 1974.

del Castillo, Richard Griswold, Teresa McKenna, and Yvonne Yarbro-Bejarano, eds. *Chicano Art. Resistance and Affirmation, 1965–1985.* Los Angeles: Wight Art Gallery, University of California, 1991.

Dickey, Roland F. *New Mexico Village Arts.* Albuquerque: University of New Mexico Press, 1949.

Dorst, John D. *The Written Suburb. An American Site, An Ethnographic Dilemma.* Philadelphia: University of Pennsylvania Press, 1989.

Eco, Umberto. *Travels in Hyper Reality: Essays.* Translated from the Italian by William Weaver. San Diego: Harcourt Brace Jovanovich, 1986.

Egri, Kit. "The Adventurous Tale of How a Noble Corpse Reached a Taos Studio." *Horse Fly* 4, no. 41 (December 1951): sec. 2.

El Independiente, 23 August 1974. New Mexico.

Eldredge, Charles, Julie Schimmel, and William Truettner. *Art in New Mexico, 1900–1945. Paths to Taos and Santa Fe.* Washington, D.C.: National Museum of American Art and Abbeville Press, 1986.

Espinosa, José E. *Saints in the Valleys. Christian Sacred Images in the History, Life and Folk Art of Spanish New Mexico.* Albuquerque: University of New Mexico Press, 1960. Rev. ed., Albuquerque: University of New Mexico Press, 1967.

Evans-Pritchard, Deirdre. "How 'They' See 'Us.' Native American Images of Tourists. In *Annals of Tourism Research* 16, no. 1 (1989): 89–105.

Ewing, Virginia Hunter. "Some Memories Concerning New Mexico's WPA—Federal Art Project." Unpublished MS, 1988.

Fischer, Michael M. J. "Ethnicity and the Post-Modern Arts of Memory." In *Writing Culture. The Poetics and Politics of Ethnography,* edited by James Clifford and George E. Marcus, 194–233. Berkeley and Los Angeles: University of California Press, 1986.

Forrest, Suzanne. *The Preservation of the Village. New Mexico's Hispanics and the New Deal.* Albuquerque: University of New Mexico Press, 1989.

Frankel, Dextra, Thomas Mercer Hartman, and the Albuquerque Museum. One Space/Three Visions. Albuquerque: Albuquerque Museum, 1979.

Gaither, James Mann. "A Return to the Village: A Study of Santa Fe and Taos, New Mexico as Cultural Centers, 1900–1934." Ph.D. diss., University of Minnesota, 1957.

Geertz, Clifford. "Art as a Cultural System." *Modern Language Notes* 91, no. 6 (1976): 1473–99.

    Local Knowledge: Further Essays in Interpretive Anthropology. New York: Basic Books, 1983.

Gibson, Arrell Morgan. *The Santa Fe and Taos Colonies: Age of the Muses, 1900–1942.* Norman: University of Oklahoma Press, 1983.

Giffords, Gloria Kay. *Mexican Folk Retablos. Masterpieces on Tin.* Tucson: University of Arizona Press, 1974.

Glassie, Henry. *Pattern in the Material Folk Culture of the Eastern United States.* Philadelphia: University of

Pennsylvania Press, 1968.

"Folk Art." In *Folklore and Folklife. An Introduction*, edited by Richard M. Dorson, pp. 253–81. Chicago: University of Chicago Press, 1972.

"Structure and Function, Folklore and the Artifact." *Semiotica* 7, no. 4 (1973): 313–51.

Passing the Time in Balleymenone: Culture and History of an Ulster Community. Philadelphia: University of Pennsylvania Press, 1982.

The Spirit of Folk Art. New York: Harry N. Abrams, Museum of International Folk Art, 1989.

Turkish Traditional Art Today. Bloomington: Indiana University Press, 1993.

Goldwater, Robert. *Primitivism in Modern Art.* New York: Random House, 1938. Enl. ed., Cambridge: Harvard University Press, Belknap Press, 1986.

Graburn, Nelson H. H., ed. *Ethnic and Tourist Arts: Cultural Expressions of the Fourth World.* Berkeley and Los Angeles: University of California Press, 1979.

Greenwood, Phaedra. "The Mother, the Struggle, the Search, the Heart. The story of Patrocinio Barela." *New Mexico Craft* 3, no. 1 (1980): 13–16.

Griego y Maestas, José. "A New Generation of Santeros." *New Mexico Magazine* 60, no. 8 (1982): 24–32.

Handler, Richard. *Nationalism and the Politics of Culture in Quebec.* Madison: University of Wisconsin Press, 1988.

Handler, Richard, and Jocelyn Linnekin. "Tradition, Genuine or Spurious." *Journal of American Folklore* 97, no. 385 (1984): 273–90.

Harris, Neil. "Museums, Merchandising, and Popular Taste: The Struggle for Influence." In *Material Culture and the Study of American Life*, edited by Ian M. G. Quimby, 140–74. New

York: W. W. Norton, 1978.

Hillerman, Anne. "The New Santeros." *Santa Fe New Mexican*, 23 October 1977, pp. 5–6.

Hunter, Russell Vernon. Papers. Archives of American Art. Smithsonian Institution, 1923–79.

"Anatomy of God." Russell Vernon Hunter Papers. Archives of American Art, Smithsonian Institution, 1942.

"Latin-American Art in USA." *Design*, 1943, pp. 20–21.

"Concerning Patrocinio Barela." In *Art for the Millions. Essays from the 1930s by Artists and Administrators of the WPA Federal Art Project*, edited and with an Introduction by Francis V. O'Connor, 96, 98–99. 1937. Reprint, Boston: New York Graphic Society, 1975.

Jaramillo, Cleofas M. *Shadows of the Past.* 1941. 2d ed., Santa Fe: Ancient City Press 1972.

Jones, Michael Owen. *The Handmade Object and Its Maker.* Berkeley and Los Angeles: University of California Press, 1975. Rev. ed., Lexington: University Press of Kentucky, 1989.

"The Concept of the `Aesthetic' in Traditional Arts." *Western Folklore* 30, no. 2 (1977): 77–104.

Kalb, Laurie Beth. *Santos, Statues and Sculpture: Contemporary Woodcarving in New Mexico.* Los Angeles: Craft and Folk Art Museum, 1988.

Karp, Ivan, and Steven D. Lavine, eds. *Exhibiting Cultures. The Poetics and Politics of Museum Display.* Washington, D.C.: Smithsonian Institution Press, 1991.

Kay, Elizabeth Althea. *Chimayó Valley Traditions.* Santa Fe: Ancient City Press, 1987.

Kienholz, Lynn, and Ira Gusalimian. Audiotape of interview by Lynn Kienholz and Ira Gusalimian with Luis Tapia, Félix López, and Laurie Beth Kalb, during exhibition, "Santos, Statues, and Sculpture," at Craft &

Folk Art Museum, Los Angeles. Los Angeles: KCRW 89.9 FM, National Public Radio, Arts L.A., 25 July 1988.

Kirshenblatt-Gimblett, Barbara. "Authenticity and Authority in the Representation of Culture: The Poetics and Politics of Tourist Production." In *Kulturkontakt/Kulturkonflikt: Zur Erfahrung des Fremden*, edited by Ina-Maria Greverus, Konrad Kostlin, and Heinz Schilling. *Notizen* 28, no. 1 (October 1988): 59–69.

"Objects of Ethnography." In *Exhibiting Cultures. The Poetics and Politics of Museum Display*, edited by Ivan Karp and Steven D. Lavine, 386–443. Washington: Smithsonian Institution Press, 1991.

Kubler, George. *The Religious Architecture of New Mexico in the Colonial Period and Since the American Occupation.* Colorado Springs: Taylor Museum of the Colorado Springs Fine Arts Center, 1940; Albuquerque: University of New Mexico Press for the School of American Research, 1972.

Kurwin, Liza, and Andrew Connors. Videotaped interview with Leo Salazar. National Museum of American Art, Smithsonian Institution, Washington, D.C. 1987.

Lange, Yvonne. "Lithography, an Agent of Technological Change in Religious Folk Art: A Thesis." *Western Folklore* 33, no. 1 (1974): 51–64.

"Santos: The Household Wooden Saints of Puerto Rico." Ph.D. diss., University of Pennsylvania, 1975.

LeFree, Betty. *Santa Clara Pottery Today.* Albuquerque: University of New Mexico Press, 1975.

Lieu, Jocelyn. "Prayers Help, Santero Says in Describing Craft." *Rio Grande Sun*, 31 March 1983.

Lippard, Lucy R. *Mixed Blessings. New Art in a Multicultural America.* New York: Pantheon Books, 1990.

López, José Benjamín. "A Perspective on the Work of Patrocinio Barela."

Unpublished MS, 1980.

    "Patrocinio Barela." Unpublished MS, 1980.

Lovasik, Rev. Lawrence G., S.V.D. *New Picture Book of Saints: Illustrated Lives of the Saints for Young and Old.* 1962. St. Joseph edition, New York: Catholic Book Publishing, 1981.

Lowenthal, David. "Age and Artifact. Dilemmas of Appreciation." In *The Interpretation of Ordinary Landscapes. Geographical Essays,* edited by D. W. Meinig, 103–28. New York: Oxford University Press, 1979.

Luhan, Mabel Dodge. "A Bridge Between Cultures." *Theatre Arts Monthly* 9, no. 5 (1925): 297–301.

    Edge of Taos Desert: An Escape to Reality. Originally published as vol. 4 of *Intimate Memories.* New York: Harcourt, Brace, 1937. Reprint, with introduction by Lois Palken Rudnick and forward by John Collier, Jr., Albuquerque: University of New Mexico Press, 1987.

MacCannell, Dean. *The Tourist. A New Theory of the Leisure Class.* New York: Schocken Books, 1976. Reprint, with introduction by Dean MacCannell, New York: Schocken Books, 1989.

MacCannell, Dean, ed. *Semiotics of Tourism.* Annals of Tourism Research. Vol. 16, no. 1. New York: Pergamon Press, 1989.

Manchester, John. Papers. Harwood Foundation Library, Taos, New Mexico, 1978.

Martínez, Eluid Lovi. *What is a New Mexico Santo?* Santa Fe: Sunstone Press, 1978.

McKay, Mary Terrence. "It's Up to the Anglos." *Southwest Profile* 13, no. 6 (1990): 34–36.

Metcalf, Eugene W., Jr. "The Politics of the Past in American Folk Art History." In *Folk Art and Art Worlds,* edited by John Michael Vlach and Simon Bronner, 27–50. Ann Arbor: UMI Research Press, 1986.

Metraux, Alfred. *Voodoo in Haiti.* Translated by Hugo Charteris. New York: Schocken Books, 1959. Reprint, with new introduction by Sidney W. Mintz, New York: Schocken Books, 1972.

Mills, George. *The People of the Saints.* Colorado Springs: Taylor Museum of the Colorado Springs Fine Arts Center, 1967.

Minge, Ward Alan. "*Efectos del Pais:* A History of Weaving Along the Rio Grande." In *Spanish Textile Tradition of New Mexico and Colorado,* compiled and edited by Nora Fisher, 8–28. Santa Fe: Museum of New Mexico Press, 1979.

Morrill, Claire. *A Taos Mosaic. Portrait of a New Mexico Village.* Albuquerque: University of New Mexico Press, 1973.

Nestor, Sarah. *The Native Market of the Spanish New Mexican Craftsmen in Santa Fe, 1933–1940.* Santa Fe: Colonial New Mexico Historical Foundation, 1978.

Nichols, John. *The Milagro Beanfield War.* New York: Ballantine Books, 1974.

Otis, Raymond. *Miguel of the Bright Mountain.* London: Victor Gollancz, 1930; Albuquerque: University of New Mexico Press, 1977.

Parezo, Nancy J. *Navajo Sandpainting: From Religious Act to Commercial Art.* Tucson: University of Arizona Press, 1983.

"Patrocinio Barela: Talented Wood Carver." *Taos News,* 29 October 1964.

Pearce, T. M. *New Mexico Place Names: A Geographical Dictionary.* Albuquerque: University of New Mexico Press, 1965. Reprint, with corrections, Albuquerque: University of New Mexico Press, 1975.

Price, Sally. *Primitive Art in Civilized Places.* Chicago: University of Chicago Press, 1989.

Quimby, Ian M. G., and Scott T. Swank, eds. *Perspectives on American Folk Art.* New York: W. W. Norton,

Winterthur Museum, 1980.

Rabinow, Paul. "Representations are Social Facts: Modernity and Post-Modernity in Anthropology." In *Writing Culture. The Poetics and Politics of Ethnography,* edited by James Clifford and George E. Marcus, 234–61. Berkeley and Los Angeles: University of California Press, 1986.

Reeve, Kay Aiken. "The Making of an American Place: The Development of Santa Fe and Taos, New Mexico as an American Cultural Center, 1898–1942." Ph.D. diss., Texas A & M University, 1977.

Robertson, Edna, and Sarah Nestor. *Artists of the Canyons and Caminos: Santa Fe, The Early Years.* Salt Lake City: Gibbs M. Smith, 1982.

Rodríguez, Sylvia. "Land, Water, and Ethnic Identity in Taos." In *Land, Water, and Culture. New Perspectives on Hispanic Land Grants,* edited by Charles L. Briggs and John R. Van Ness, 313–403. Albuquerque: University of New Mexico Press, 1987.

Rosenak, Chuck. *Museum of American Folk Art Encyclopedia of Twentieth-Century American Folk Art and Artists.* New York: Abbeville Press, 1990.

Rosenbaum, Robert J., and Robert W. Larson. "Mexicano Resistance to the Expropriation of Grant Lands in New Mexico." In *Land, Water, and Culture. New Perspectives on Hispanic Land Grants,* edited by Charles L. Briggs and John R. Van Ness, 269–310. Albuquerque: University of New Mexico Press, 1987.

Rudnick, Lois Palken. *Mabel Dodge Luhan. New Woman, New Worlds.* Albuquerque: University of New Mexico Press, 1984.

    "Re-Naming the Land. Anglo Expatriate Women in the Southwest." In *The Desert is No Lady. Southwest-*

ern Landscapes in Women's Writing and Art, edited by Vera Norwood and Janice Monk, 10–27. New Haven: Yale University Press, 1987.

Sagel, Jim. "Burro Ride Offers View, 300 Years of History." Journal North, 4 July 1984, p. E-4.

Said, Edward W. Orientalism. New York: Vintage Books, 1978.

Santos de New Mexico. San Francisco: Galeria de la Raza, 1983.

Schimmel, Julie. "From Salon to Pueblo: The First Generation." In Art in New Mexico, 1900–1945. Paths to Taos and Santa Fe. Washington, D.C.: National Museum of American Art and Abbeville Press, 1986.

Shalkop, Robert L. Arroyo Hondo: The Folk Art of a New Mexican Village. Colorado Springs: Taylor Museum of the Colorado Springs Fine Arts Center, 1969.

Sources and Inspirations: Paintings by Paul Pletka. Santa Fe: Museum of Fine Arts, Museum of New Mexico, 1990.

Steele, Thomas J., S. J. Santos and Saints: The Religious Folk Art of Hispanic New Mexico. Albuquerque: Calvin Horn, 1974. Reprint, Santa Fe: Ancient City Press, 1982.

Steele, Thomas J., S. J., and Rowena A. Rivera. Penitente Self-Government: Brotherhoods and Councils, 1797–1947. Santa Fe: Ancient City Press, 1985.

Stewart, Susan. On Longing. Narratives of the Miniature, the Gigantic, the Souvenir, the Collection. Baltimore: Johns Hopkins University Press, 1984.

Stoller, Marianne L. "'Peregrinas' with Many Visions." In The Desert is No Lady. Southwestern Landscapes in Women's Writing and Art, edited by Vera Norwood and Janice Monk, 125–46. New Haven: Yale University Press, 1987.

Sturiale, Paul. "Artists Work to Save Heritage." Santa Fe New Mexican, [1978].

Sweeney, James Johnson. Henry Moore.

New York: Museum of Modern Art, 1946.

Taylor, Lonn, and Dessa Bokides. New Mexican Furniture, 1600–1940. The Origins, Survival, and Revival of Furniture Making in the Hispanic Southwest. Santa Fe: Museum of New Mexico Press, 1987.

Turner, Victor W., and Edward M. Bruner, eds. The Anthropology of Experience. Urbana: University of Illinois Press, 1986.

Udall, Sharyn R. Modernist Painting in New Mexico 1913–1935. Albuquerque: University of New Mexico Press, 1984.

_____. Santa Fe Art Colony 1900–1942. Santa Fe: Gerald Peters Gallery, 1987.

_____. "The Case for an Innocent Eye." Antiques & Fine Art, 1988, pp. 86–93.

Vedder, Ann. "History of the Spanish Colonial Arts Society, Inc., 1951–1981." In Hispanic Arts and Ethnohistory in the Southwest. New Papers Inspired by the Work of E. Boyd, edited by Marta Weigle with Claudia Larcombe and Samuel Larcombe, 205–17. Santa Fe: Ancient City Press, 1983.

Vlach, John Michael. "American Folk Art: Questions and Quandaries." Winterthur Portfolio 15, no. 4 (1980): 345–55.

Vlach, John Michael, and Simon J. Bronner, eds. Folk Art and Art Worlds. Ann Arbor: UMI Research Press, 1986.

Wallrich, William J. "The Santero Tradition in the San Luis Valley." Western Folklore 10 (1951): 153–61.

Waters, Frank. People of the Valley. Denver: Sage Books, 1941.

Weigle, Marta. Hispanic Villages of Northern New Mexico. A Reprint of Volume II of The 1935 Tewa Basin Study, with Supplementary Materials. Santa Fe: Lightning Tree Press, 1975.

_____. Brothers of Light, Brothers of Blood. The Penitentes of the Southwest. Santa Fe: Ancient City Press, 1976.

_____. "The First Twenty-Five Years of the Spanish Colonial Arts Society." In Hispanic Arts and Ethnohistory in the Southwest. New Papers Inspired by the Work of E. Boyd. edited by Marta Weigle with Claudia Larcombe and Samuel Larcombe, 181–203. Santa Fe: Ancient City Press, 1983.

_____. "Dancer, Pilgrim, Trader and Tourist in the Development of a Southwestern Folklore." Unpublished MS. presented at the annual American Folklore Society meetings, 1983.

Weigle, Marta, and Kyle Fiore. Santa Fe and Taos. The Writer's Era, 1916–1941. Santa Fe: Ancient City Press, 1982.

Weigle, Marta, with Claudia Larcombe and Samuel Larcombe, eds. Hispanic Arts and Ethnohistory in the Southwest. New Papers Inspired by the Work of E. Boyd. Santa Fe: Ancient City Press, 1983.

Wilder, Mitchell A., and Edgar Breitenbach, eds. Santos: The Religious Folk Art of New Mexico. Colorado Springs: Taylor Museum of the Colorado Springs Fine Arts Center, 1943.

Williams, Raymond. Marxism and Literature. Oxford: Oxford University Press, 1977.

The Wingspread Collector's Guide: Santa Fe and Taos. Albuquerque: Wingspread Communications, 1988.

The Wingspread Collector's Guide: Santa Fe and Taos. Vol. 5, no. 1. Albuquerque: Wingspread Incorporated, 1991.

Winkelhorst, Michael. "Edward González: Artist on the Attack." Santa Fe Reporter 16, no. 6 (1–7 August 1990): 1, 11–12.

WPA Guide to 1930s New Mexico. Originally published as New Mexico, A Guide to the Colorful State. New York: Hastings House, 1940. Reprint, with foreword by Marc Simmons, Tucson: University of Arizona Press, 1989.

Wroth, William. Christian Images in Hispanic New Mexico. Colorado

Springs: Taylor Museum of the
Colorado Springs Fine Arts Center,
1982.

  "New Hope in Hard Times:
Hispanic Crafts are Revived During
Troubled Years." *El Palacio* 89, no. 2
(1983): 22–31.

  *Furniture from the Hispanic
Southwest.* Santa Fe: Ancient City
Press, 1984.

  ed. *Hispanic Crafts of the
Southwest.* Colorado Springs: Taylor
Museum of the Colorado Springs
Fine Arts Center, 1977.

Ybarra-Frausto, Tomás. "The Chicano
Movement/The Movement of
Chicano Art." In *Exhibiting Cultures.
The Poetics and Politics of Museum
Display,* edited by Ivan Karp and
Steven D. Lavine, 128–50. Washing-
ton, D.C.: Smithsonian Institution
Press, 1991.

Yoder, Don. "Official Religion versus Folk
Religion." *Pennsylvania Folklife,*
1965–66, pp. 36–52.

Yoder, Don, ed. Folk Religion: A Sympo-
sium. *Western Folklore* 33, no. 1
(1974): special issue.

  "Toward a Definition of Folk
Religion." *Western Folklore* 33, no. 1
(1974): 2–15.

INDEX